America's Best
A Collection of Savory Recipes™

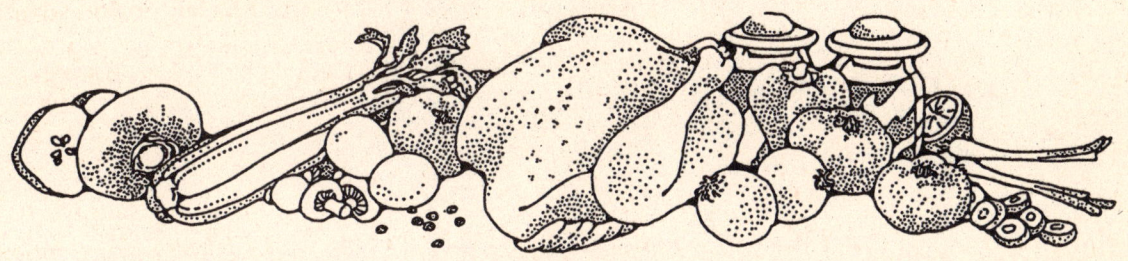

Volume 1

® Landoll, Inc.
Ashland, Ohio 44805
Created and manufactured by arrangement with Ideals Publishing Corp.
Copyright © MCMLXXXV by Ideals Publishing Corp.
All rights reserved.
Manufactured in the United States of America.

Contents

Breads 4
Cakes & Pies 16
Cookies 29
Desserts 44
Meat 65
Rolls & Muffins 75
Sauces, Dips & Dressings 81
Soups & Salads 86
Vegetables & Rice 97
Menus 106

Breads

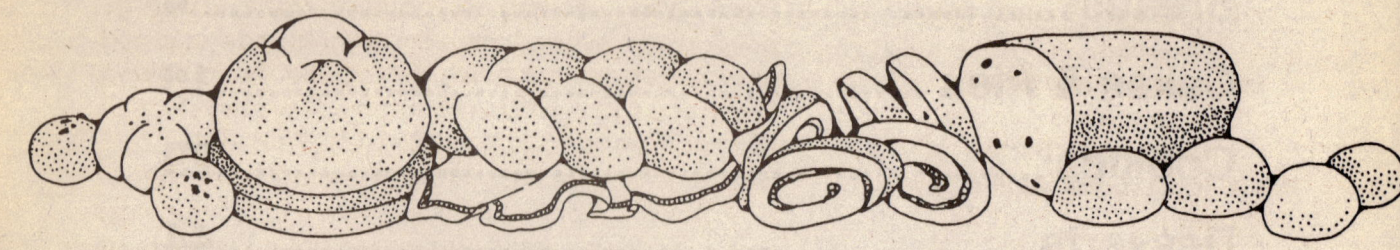

SEASONED BREAD STICKS

Makes 8 sticks

2 tablespoons butter or margarine, melted
¼ teaspoon crushed dried basil
¼ teaspoon crushed dried oregano
1 package refrigerated bread sticks

Combine butter, basil and oregano. Prepare bread sticks for baking; brush with butter mixture. Bake at 350° for 15 to 18 minutes or until lightly browned.

Pumpkin Bread

Makes 2 loaves

3 cups sugar
1 cup vegetable oil
4 eggs, lightly beaten
2 cups canned pumpkin
3½ cups flour
2 teaspoons baking soda
1 teaspoon baking powder
1 teaspoon salt
1 teaspoon nutmeg
1 teaspoon ground allspice
1 teaspoon ground cinnamon
½ teaspoon ground cloves
⅔ cup water

In a large mixing bowl, combine sugar, oil, eggs, and pumpkin; blend well. In a separate bowl, combine flour, baking soda, baking powder, salt, nutmeg, allspice, cinnamon, and cloves. Alternately add flour mixture and water to pumpkin mixture, beginning and ending with flour; blend well after each addition. Pour batter into two greased 9 x 5-inch loaf pans. Bake in a preheated 350° F. oven 1½ hours or until a wooden pick inserted in the center comes out clean. Cool in pans 10 minutes. Invert onto a wire rack to cool completely.

Breads

Date Bread
Makes 1 loaf

- 1 package (2 cups) dates, chopped
- 1½ cups boiling water
- 2 cups sugar
- 1 tablespoon butter
- 1 tablespoon vanilla
- 1 egg
- 3 cups flour
- 2 teaspoons baking soda
- 1 teaspoon salt
- 1 cup chopped pecans

Place dates in boiling water and set aside. In a large bowl, cream sugar, butter, and vanilla; add egg and mix well. In another bowl, stir together flour, baking soda, and salt. Add flour to creamed mixture; stir until just moistened. Drain dates well. Add dates and pecans to dough. Pour into a greased 9 x 5-inch loaf pan. Bake in a preheated 400° F. oven for 15 minutes; then turn down heat to 300° F. and bake 1½ hours or until a wooden pick inserted in the center comes out clean. Let bread cool in pan 10 minutes. Invert on wire rack and let cool completely.

Good Egg Bread
Makes 3 loaves

- 1½ cups scalded milk
- ½ cup butter
- 2 teaspoons salt
- ½ cup sugar
- 2 packages yeast
- ½ cup lukewarm water
- 2 beaten eggs
- 8 cups flour

Pour scalded milk over butter, salt, and sugar. Cool. Dissolve yeast in lukewarm water and let stand until it bubbles, about 5 minutes. Add yeast and beaten eggs to cooled milk. Gradually add flour, beating thoroughly. Use only enough flour to make a soft dough. Turn out on a lightly floured board and knead until smooth and elastic. Place in a greased bowl, cover, and let rise 1½ hours or until doubled in bulk. Punch down dough and shape into 3 loaves. Place in greased 8-inch loaf pans. Cover and let rise until dough is doubled in bulk. Bake in a preheated 425° F. oven for 10 minutes, then bake at 350° F. for 40 minutes more or until bread sounds hollow when tapped on the bottom.

Breads

Raisin Braid
Makes 1 braid

3½ to 4 cups flour
1 package active dry yeast
¼ cup sugar
¼ teaspoon salt
1 cup whipping cream, lukewarm
2 eggs
1 egg white
1 teaspoon vanilla
1½ cups raisins
1 egg yolk
2 tablespoons milk

Sift flour into a large bowl. Sprinkle yeast onto flour; mix together. Blend in sugar, salt, cream, eggs, egg white, and vanilla. If dough becomes sticky, add flour, but dough must remain moderately soft. Place on a lightly floured board and knead until smooth. Place dough in a greased bowl; turn once to grease lightly. Cover and let rise 1½ hours or until doubled in bulk. Punch down dough. Turn out onto a lightly floured board and knead in raisins. Shape ⅔ of the dough into 3 rolls, each about 12 inches long. Braid the rolls together; place on a greased 10 x 15-inch cookie sheet. Beat egg yolk and milk together in a small bowl. Press a hollow along along the length of the braid with a rolling pin. Brush the hollow with the egg yolk mixture. From the remaining dough, form 3 rolls, each about 10 inches long; braid them together. Place this braid atop the hollow of the larger braid; brush with egg yolk mixture. Cover and let rise 45 minutes or until doubled in bulk. Bake in a preheated 375° F. oven 35 minutes or until golden brown and bottom sounds hollow when tapped. Remove from pan and cool on wire rack.

Herb Bread
Makes 1 loaf

½ to ⅔ cup soft butter
2 teaspoons finely chopped onion
1 teaspoon chopped fresh parsley
1 teaspoon basil
1 teaspoon lemon juice
1 loaf of bread sliced ¾ through

Mix the first 5 ingredients and spread on the bread slices. Heat on a cookie sheet at 250° F. for 25 minutes. Separate slices before serving.

Breads

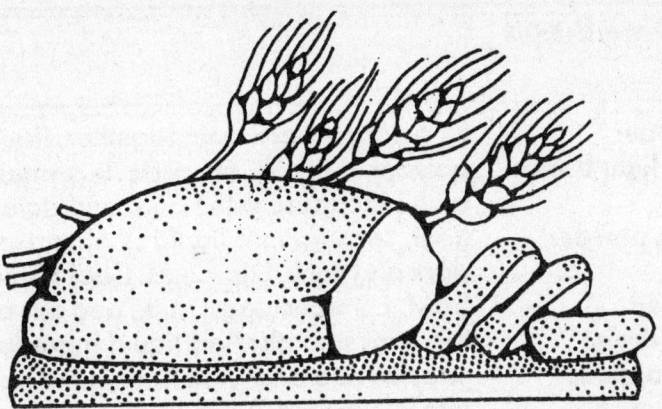

Lemon Bread
Makes 1 loaf

- 3 tablespoons margarine
- 1 cup sugar
- ½ teaspoon salt
- 2 eggs
- 1½ cups sifted flour
- 1 teaspoon baking powder
- ½ cup milk
- 1 tablespoon grated lemon peel
- Juice of 1 lemon
- ½ cup sugar

In a small bowl, cream margarine, sugar, and salt. Add egg, and set aside. In another bowl, stir together flour and baking powder. Add flour and milk alternately to creamed mixture, mixing well after each addition. Add lemon peel; pour batter into a greased 9 x 5-inch loaf pan. Bake in a preheated 350° F. oven for 55 minutes or until a wooden pick inserted in the center comes out clean. In a saucepan, heat lemon juice and sugar until sugar dissolves. Remove loaf from pan while still hot, and drizzle lemon mixture over the top.

Wheat Germ Bread
Makes 1 loaf

- 2¾ cups all-purpose flour, divided
- 2 packages dry yeast
- ½ cup wheat germ
- 1½ teaspoons salt
- 1 cup warm water
- ¼ cup molasses
- 2 tablespoons shortening
- 1 egg

In a large bowl, mix 1½ cups flour, yeast, wheat germ, and salt. Add water, molasses, shortening, and egg; mix again. Gradually stir in remaining flour to make a stiff dough. Cover; let rise until double in bulk, about 1 hour. Punch down dough. Place in greased 9-inch loaf pan or 2-quart casserole. Cover and let rise about 45 minutes. Bake in preheated 375° F. oven 35 to 50 minutes or until deep golden brown. Remove from pan and cool before slicing.

Breads

Dark Pineapple Date Bread
Makes 1 loaf

- 2 cups all-purpose flour
- ¼ cup firmly packed light brown sugar
- 1 tablespoon baking powder
- 1 teaspoon salt
- 1 8-ounce can crushed pineapple (do not drain)
- 1¼ cups (8 ounces) chopped, pitted dates
- 1 cup chopped pecans
- 2 eggs
- ⅔ cup milk
- ¼ cup vegetable oil

In a large bowl, stir together flour, sugar, baking powder, and salt; set aside. In a small saucepan combine pineapple with liquid and dates; cook over low heat, stirring until liquid is absorbed and mixture is dark and thick. Stir in nuts. Cool 10 minutes. In another bowl, combine eggs, milk, and oil; add date mixture. Stir until smooth. Add liquid ingredients to flour mixture, stirring only until flour is moistened. Pour batter into a greased 9 x 5-inch loaf pan. Bake in a preheated 350° F. oven 60 to 70 minutes. Cover pan with foil the last 15 minutes of baking to prevent excessive browning. Cool 10 minutes in pan. Invert onto wire rack to cool completely.

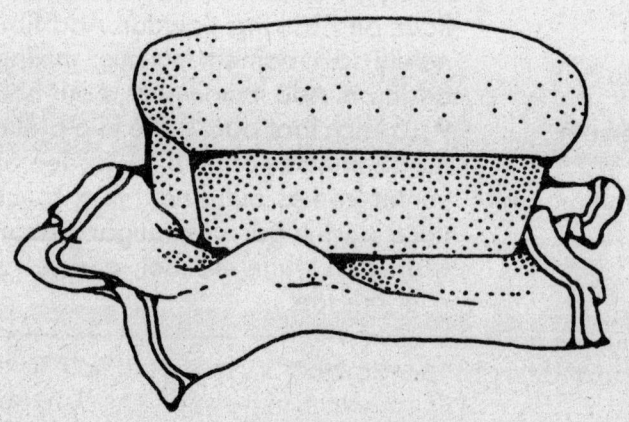

ITALIAN TOAST SLICES
Makes 12 slices

- ½ cup butter *or* margarine, softened
- ¼ cup grated Parmesan cheese
- 1 teaspoon crushed dried oregano
- 12 slices Italian bread

Preheat broiler. Combine butter, Parmesan and oregano; spread on one side of each bread slice. Place bread, buttered-side-up, on a baking sheet. Broil 2 to 3 inches from heat for 1 to 2 minutes or until toasted.

Breads

Mini-Loaves
Makes 4 mini-loaves

- 4 to 5 cups all-purpose flour, divided
- 2 packages dry yeast
- ¾ cup milk
- 1 cup water
- 2 tablespoons shortening
- 2 tablespoons sugar
- 2 teaspoons salt
- 1 egg
- Melted butter, optional

Into a large mixing bowl, measure 2 cups flour; add yeast and mix. In a small saucepan, mix milk, water, shortening, sugar, and salt; heat until warm (120° to 130° F.). Pour into the flour-yeast mixture. Add egg and mix well. Gradually stir in enough of remaining flour to form a soft dough. Knead 5 to 10 minutes, until mixture is smooth. Cover dough and let rest 20 minutes. Divide dough into 4 equal parts. Shape into small loaves. Place in four 3 x 5 x 2-inch pans. Let rise until double in bulk, about 45 minutes. Bake 25 to 35 minutes in a preheated 400° F. oven. Remove from pans, and cool on racks. Brush with butter for soft crust, if desired.

Hearth Bread
Makes 2 large loaves

- 6 to 6½ cups all-purpose flour
- 2 packages dry yeast
- 2 cups water
- 2 tablespoons sugar
- 2 teaspoons salt
- 1 egg white, beaten
- 2 tablespoons water
- Cornmeal

Stir together 2 cups flour and the yeast. In a saucepan, heat water, sugar, and salt until warm, 120° to 130° F. Add liquid ingredients to flour-yeast mixture and beat until smooth. Gradually add remaining flour to make a moderately stiff dough. Turn onto lightly floured surface; knead until smooth and elastic, 12 to 15 minutes. Cover dough and let rise 40 minutes. Punch down. Form into 2 loaves. Place on greased baking sheet, seam side down. With sharp knife, make diagonal cuts across top of loaves. Combine egg and water; brush on loaves. Sprinkle lightly with cornmeal. Let rise until double in bulk, about 20 to 30 minutes. Bake in preheated 375° F. oven 45 to 50 minutes. Brush tops with hot water after 20 minutes of baking; brush with water every 10 minutes until done.

Breads

Cheese Bread
Makes 1 loaf

- 1 package active dry yeast
- 1 teaspoon sugar
- 1 cup lukewarm water
- 3 to 3½ cups wheat flour
- 1 teaspoon salt
- ⅛ teaspoon ground black pepper
- 3 tablespoons vegetable oil
- ¾ cup Emmenthaler cheese, cut into small cubes
- ⅓ cup Emmenthaler cheese, cut into wedges
- 1 egg yolk
- 1 tablespoon water

Sprinkle yeast and sugar in ½ cup of the lukewarm water; set aside for 5 minutes. Into a large bowl, sift flour, add salt and pepper. Pour in yeast mixture, remaining water, and oil. Mix well. If the dough is sticky, add a little flour, but dough must remain moderately soft. Place dough on a lightly floured board and knead until smooth. Place dough in a greased bowl; turn once to grease lightly. Cover and let rise 1½ hours or until doubled in bulk. Punch down dough. Place on pastry board and knead in the cubes of cheese until dough is smooth. Shape into a circle and place in an 8-inch greased soufflé dish. Insert cheese wedges into the dough. Cover and let rise 45 minutes or until doubled in bulk. In a small bowl, mix egg yolk and water. Brush top of bread with egg glaze. Bake in a preheated 400° F. oven 50 minutes or until bottom sounds hollow when tapped. Remove bread from dish; cool on wire rack.

Applesauce Nut Bread
Makes 1 loaf

- 2 cups flour
- ¾ cup sugar
- 1 tablespoon baking powder
- 1 teaspoon salt
- ½ teaspoon baking soda
- ½ teaspoon ground cinnamon
- 1 egg, lightly beaten
- 1 cup applesauce
- 2 tablespoons vegetable shortening, melted
- 1 cup chopped nuts

In a bowl, sift together flour, sugar, baking powder, salt, baking soda, and cinnamon; set aside. In another bowl, combine egg, applesauce, and melted shortening; blend well. Gradually add flour mixture; blend well. Stir in nuts. Turn batter into a greased 9 x 5-inch loaf pan. Bake in a preheated 350° F. oven 1 hour or until a wooden pick inserted in the center comes out clean. Cool in pan 10 minutes. Invert onto a wire rack to cool completely.

Breads

Almond Bread
Makes 1 loaf

3½ to 4 cups flour
1 package active dry yeast
⅓ cup sugar
¼ teaspoon salt
1 cup whipping cream, lukewarm
⅓ cup butter *or* margarine, melted and cooled to lukewarm
1 egg
1 teaspoon vanilla
1 cup raisins
1 cup almonds

Into a large bowl, sift flour; add yeast and mix. Blend in sugar, salt, cream, butter, egg, and vanilla. If dough becomes sticky, add flour, but dough must remain moderately soft. Place on a lightly floured board and knead until smooth. Place in a greased bowl; turn once to grease lightly. Cover and let rise 1½ hours or until doubled in bulk. Punch down dough. Turn out onto lightly floured board and knead until smooth. Knead in raisins and almonds. Shape dough into a loaf; place in a greased 9 x 5 x 3-inch loaf pan. Cover and let rise 45 minutes or until doubled in bulk. Brush loaf with water and bake in a preheated 375° F. oven for 35 minutes or until golden brown and bottom sounds hollow when tapped. Brush with water immediately after baking. Remove from pan and cool on wire rack.

Cinnamon Coffee Round
Makes 1 coffee cake

¾ cup sugar
6 tablespoons vegetable shortening
1 egg
2 cups flour
2 teaspoons baking powder
1 teaspoon salt
1 cup milk
Streusel Topping

In a mixing bowl, cream sugar and shortening until light and fluffy. Beat in egg. In a separate bowl, sift together flour, baking powder, and salt. Alternately add flour mixture and milk to creamed mixture; blend well after each addition. Stir in half of the Streusel Topping. Spread batter into a greased 8-inch round baking pan. Smooth top of dough. Sprinkle with remaining Streusel Topping. Bake in a preheated 350° F. oven 30 to 35 minutes or until a wooden pick inserted in the center comes out clean. Serve warm.

Streusel Topping

½ cup sugar
2 tablespoons flour
1 tablespoon ground cinnamon
2 tablespoons butter *or* margarine, melted
¾ cup chopped nuts
⅓ cup raisins, optional

In a small bowl, combine all ingredients; stir until blended.

Breads

Sesame Twist
Makes 2 loaves

5½ to 6 cups flour, divided
2 packages (¼ ounce each) active dry yeast
1 cup milk
1 cup water
2 tablespoons sugar
2 tablespoons vegetable oil
2 teaspoons salt
1 egg white beaten with 1 tablespoon water
Sesame seed

In a large bowl, stir together 2 cups flour and yeast. In a saucepan, combine milk, water, sugar, 2 tablespoons oil, and salt; heat over low heat until very warm (120 to 130° F.). Stir liquids into flour mixture. Beat on high speed of an electric mixer 3 minutes or until smooth. Stir in enough remaining flour to make a soft dough. Turn dough out onto a lightly floured surface. Knead until smooth and elastic, 8 to 10 minutes. Cover and let rise 20 minutes. Divide dough in 4 parts. Roll each part into a 15-inch rope. Wrap 2 ropes around each other in a spiral; tuck ends under. Repeat. Place in two greased 9 x 5-inch loaf pans. Brush tops with egg white mixture. Sprinkle with sesame seed. Cover and let rise in a warm draft-free place until doubled in bulk, 30 to 45 minutes. Preheat oven to 400° F. Bake 35 to 40 minutes or until loaves sound hollow when lightly tapped. Turn out of pans onto a wire rack to cool.

GARLIC BREAD
Makes 8 slices

¼ cup butter *or* margarine, softened
¼ teaspoon garlic powder
Dash paprika
8 slices Italian bread

Combine butter, garlic powder and paprika. Spread on 1 side of each bread slice. Stack slices with buttered sides together; wrap in foil. Heat at 375°, about 15 minutes or until hot.

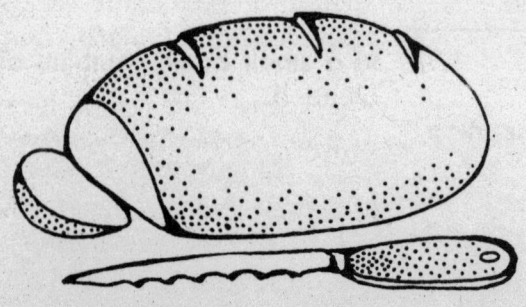

Breads

Dilly Bread
Makes 1 loaf

- 2½ to 3 cups flour, divided
- 2 tablespoons sugar
- 2 to 3 teaspoons instant minced onion
- 2 teaspoons dill seed
- 1¼ teaspoons salt
- ¼ teaspoon baking soda
- 1 package (¼ ounce) active dry yeast
- 1 carton (8 ounces) cream-style cottage cheese
- ¼ cup lukewarm water (110° F.)
- 1 tablespoon butter *or* margarine
- 1 egg
- Butter, softened

In a large mixing bowl, combine 1 cup flour, sugar, onion, dill seed, salt, baking soda, and yeast; set aside. In a saucepan, heat cottage cheese, water, and butter until very warm (120 to 130° F.). Add warm liquid and egg to flour mixture; blend on low speed of electric mixer until moistened, then beat 3 minutes at medium speed. Stir in remaining 1½ to 2 cups flour by hand to form a stiff batter. Place in a greased bowl; lightly oil top. Cover and let rise in warm, draft-free place until doubled in bulk, 45 to 65 minutes. Punch down. Turn dough into a well-greased 1½- or 2-quart casserole. Cover and let rise until doubled in bulk, 30 to 45 minutes. Preheat oven to 350° F. Bake 35 to 40 minutes or until golden. Turn out of casserole onto a wire rack to cool. Brush bread with butter while still warm.

Braided Fruit Bread
Makes 1 braid

- 3½ to 4 cups flour
- 1 package active dry yeast
- ⅓ cup sugar
- ¼ teaspoon salt
- ¾ cup sour cream at room temperature
- ½ cup milk, lukewarm
- ⅓ cup margarine, melted and cooled to lukewarm
- 1 teaspoon vanilla
- 4 slices canned pineapple, diced
- 1 cup raisins
- ½ cup flaked almonds

Into a large bowl, sift flour. Sprinkle with yeast and mix well. Blend in sugar, salt, sour cream, milk, margarine, and vanilla. Add flour if the dough is sticky, but dough must remain moderately soft. Place dough on lightly floured board and knead until smooth. Place dough in a greased bowl; turn once to grease lightly. Cover bowl and let dough rise 1½ hours or until doubled in bulk. Punch down dough. Divide into 3 equal portions. Knead pineapple into one portion, adding more flour only if needed. Knead raisins into a second portion, and almonds into the remaining portion. Shape each third into a 14-inch long roll. Braid the rolls together and place on greased 10 x 15-inch cookie sheet. Cover and let rise 45 minutes or until doubled in bulk. Brush the braid with water and bake in a preheated 375° F. oven for 35 minutes or until golden brown and bottom sounds hollow when tapped. Brush bread with water, remove from pan, and cool on wire rack.

Breads

White Bread
Makes 1 loaf

- 5½ to 6 cups all-purpose flour, divided
- 2 packages dry yeast
- 1 cup milk
- 1 cup water
- 2 tablespoons sugar
- 2 tablespoons oil
- 2 teaspoons salt
- Oil

In a bowl, stir together 2 cups flour and yeast; set aside. In a saucepan, heat milk, water, sugar, 2 tablespoons oil, and salt to lukewarm (110° F.). Add liquid ingredients to flour-yeast mixture; beat until smooth. Stir in additional remaining flour to make a soft dough. Turn onto lightly floured board and knead until smooth, about 5 to 10 minutes. Cover dough and let rest 20 minutes. Punch down and form into a loaf. Place in a greased 9-inch loaf pan; brush with oil. Let rise until double in bulk, about 30 to 45 minutes. Bake in preheated 400° F. oven 35 to 40 minutes. Remove from pan immediately; brush with oil and cool on wire rack.

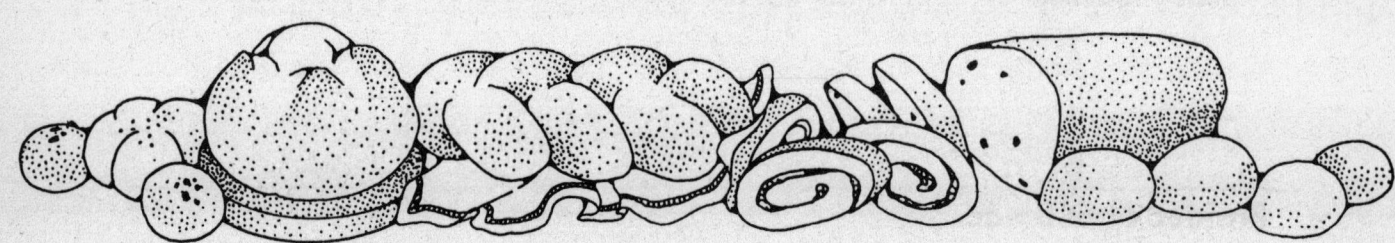

Oatmeal Bread
Makes 2 loaves

- 1 cup uncooked oatmeal
- 1 cup milk, scalded
- ½ cup boiling water
- ⅓ cup shortening
- ½ cup firmly packed brown sugar
- 2 teaspoons salt
- 2 packages dry yeast
- ½ cup warm water
- 5 cups sifted flour

In a large bowl, mix oatmeal, milk, and boiling water. Add shortening, sugar, and salt. Let stand until lukewarm. In a small bowl, sprinkle yeast on ½ cup warm water; stir until dissolved. Stir into oatmeal mixture; add half the flour and mix until smooth. Gradually add remaining flour until dough is moderately stiff. Turn out on lightly floured board and knead 7 minutes. Place dough in greased bowl, cover, and let rise 1½ hours. Punch down; knead and shape into loaves. Let rise until double in bulk. Bake at 400° F. for 10 minutes. Reduce heat to 350° F., and bake 40 minutes longer.

Breads

Apricot Bread
Makes 1 loaf

- 2 cups flour
- 1 cup sugar
- 2½ teaspoons baking powder
- ¾ teaspoon salt
- ¾ cup crunchy nut-like cereal
- ⅔ cup chopped dried apricots
- 1 egg
- 1¼ cups milk
- 2 tablespoons vegetable shortening, melted

In a large bowl, mix flour, sugar, baking powder, and salt. Stir in cereal and apricots. In a small bowl, beat together egg and milk. Stir in melted shortening. Add liquids to flour mixture; stir until evenly moist. Turn batter into a greased 9 x 5-inch loaf pan. Bake in a preheated 350° F. oven 1 hour or until a wooden pick inserted in the center comes out clean. Cool in pan 10 minutes. Invert onto a wire rack to cool completely.

Carrot Bread
Makes 1 loaf

- ¾ cup vegetable oil
- 1 cup sugar
- 2 eggs
- 1½ cups flour
- ¼ teaspoon salt
- 1 teaspoon baking soda
- 1 teaspoon ground cinnamon
- 1 cup grated carrots
- 1 cup chopped dates
- 1 cup chopped nuts

In a large bowl, combine oil, sugar, and eggs; blend well. In a separate bowl, mix together flour, salt, baking soda, and cinnamon. Alternately add flour mixture and carrots to sugar mixture; blend well after each addition. Stir in dates and nuts. Pour batter into a greased 9 x 5 inch loaf pan. Bake in a preheated 350° F. oven 1 hour or until a wooden pick inserted in the center comes out clean. Cool in pan 10 minutes. Invert onto a wire rack to cool completely.

Cakes & Pies

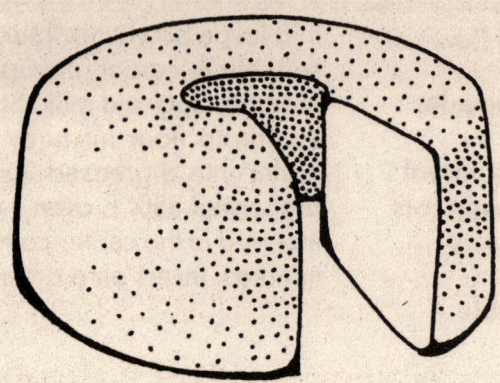

Yeast Pound Cake
Makes 1 bundt cake

- ¾ cup whipping cream, lukewarm
- 1 package active dry yeast
- 2 teaspoons sugar
- 3½ cups flour
- ¾ cup sugar
- ¾ cup ground almonds
- Peel of ½ lemon, grated
- ¾ cup butter *or* margarine, melted and cooled to lukewarm
- 3 eggs
- 1 teaspoon vanilla
- 1½ cups raisins
- 3 tablespoons slivered almonds
- Powdered sugar

Into a small bowl, pour whipping cream. Stir in yeast and 2 teaspoons sugar; set aside for 5 minutes. Into a large bowl, sift flour. Make a hollow in the center and add ¾ cup sugar, ground almonds, lemon peel, butter, eggs, vanilla, and yeast mixture; mix well. If the dough becomes sticky, add flour, but dough must remain moderately soft. Place dough on a lightly floured board; knead in raisins. Sprinkle almonds in the bottom of a greased bundt pan. Spread dough evenly in pan. Let rise 2½ hours or until doubled in bulk. Bake in a preheated 350° F. oven 40 to 45 minutes or until a wooden pick inserted in center comes out clean. Turn out cake onto wire rack to cool, dust generously with powdered sugar.

Cakes & Pies

Chocolate Dream Cake
Makes one 9 x 13-inch cake

- 1¾ cups sifted cake flour
- 1½ cups sugar
- 1 teaspoon baking soda
- 1 teaspoon salt
- ½ cup sifted cocoa
- ½ cup butter, softened
- 1 cup buttermilk, divided
- 2 eggs

In a large bowl, combine flour, sugar, baking soda, salt, and cocoa. Add butter and ⅔ cup buttermilk; mix well. Add eggs and remaining buttermilk; mix well. Pour into a greased 9 x 13-inch baking pan. Bake in a preheated 350° F. oven about 30 minutes. Cool 10 minutes. Remove from pan; cool on wire rack.

Apple Streusel Cake
Makes one 9 x 13-inch cake

- 1 cup milk, lukewarm
- 1 package active dry yeast
- 2 teaspoons sugar
- 3½ to 4 cups flour
- ¼ cup sugar
- ¼ teaspoon salt
- ¼ cup butter *or* margarine, melted and cooled to lukewarm
- 1 teaspoon vanilla
- 3½ cups peeled, thinly sliced cooking apples
- ½ cup slivered almonds
- ½ cup golden raisins
- 1 teaspoon cinnamon
- ⅛ cup sugar

Into a small bowl, pour lukewarm milk. Add yeast and sugar, stirring until dissolved; set aside for 5 minutes. Into a large bowl, sift flour. Make a hollow in the center. Add ¼ cup sugar, salt, butter, vanilla, and the yeast mixture in the hollow. Mix well. If the dough is sticky, add flour, but the dough must remain moderately soft. Place dough on a lightly floured board and knead until smooth. Place dough in a greased bowl; turn once to grease lightly. Cover and let rise 45 minutes or until doubled in bulk. Punch down dough. Pat into greased 9 x 13-inch cake pan. Arrange apple slices on top of dough. Cover and let rise 45 minutes or until doubled in bulk. Sprinkle top with almonds, raisins, cinnamon, and ⅛ cup sugar. Bake in a preheated 375° F. oven 25 to 30 minutes or until golden brown. Remove from pan; cool on wire rack. To serve, cut into 2 x 3-inch strips.

Cakes & Pies

Carrot Cake
Makes one 9 x 13-inch cake

- 2 cups flour
- 2 teaspoons baking soda
- 2 teaspoons ground cinnamon
- 1½ teaspoons salt
- 2 cups sugar
- 1½ cups vegetable oil
- 4 eggs
- 1 tablespoon vanilla
- 3 cups grated carrots
- 1 cup chopped pitted dates
- 1 cup flaked coconut
- 1 cup raisins, optional
- 1 cup chopped nuts, optional
- Cream Cheese Frosting

In a medium bowl, sift together flour, baking soda, cinnamon, and salt; set aside. In a large mixing bowl, combine sugar and oil; blend well. Beat in eggs, one at a time, until well blended. Stir in vanilla. Gradually add dry ingredients; beat until well blended. Stir in carrots, dates, coconut, raisins, and nuts, if desired. Pour batter into a greased 9 x 13-inch baking pan. Bake at 350° F. for 30 to 40 minutes or until center springs back when lightly touched. Cool on a wire rack. Frost with Cream Cheese Frosting.

Cream Cheese Frosting

- 2 packages (3 ounces each) cream cheese, softened
- 6 tablespoons butter or margarine, softened
- 1 tablespoon milk
- 1 teaspoon vanilla
- 4 cups sifted powdered sugar

In a mixing bowl, combine cream cheese and butter; cream with electric mixer until light and fluffy. Beat in milk and vanilla. Gradually beat in powdered sugar until of spreading consistency.

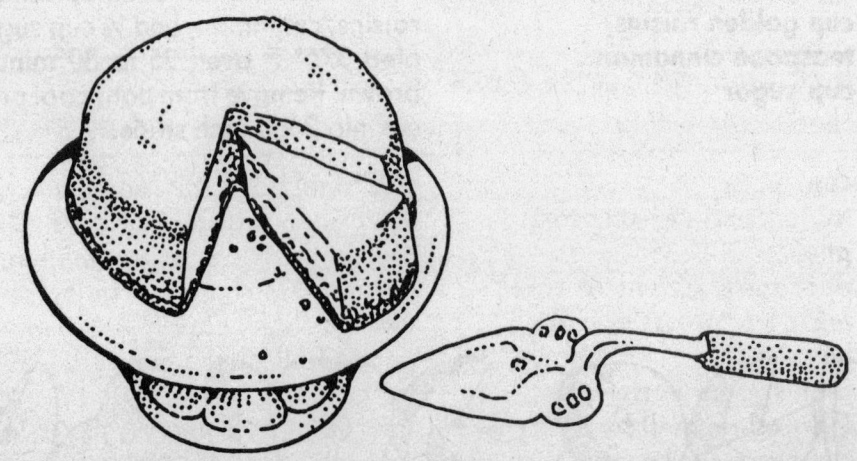

Cakes & Pies

Honey Cake
Makes one 8-inch cake

- ½ cup sugar
- ½ cup butter *or* margarine
- 2 eggs
- ½ cup honey
- ¾ cup milk
- 1 teaspoon almond flavoring
- 2 cups flour
- 2½ teaspoons baking powder
- ½ teaspoon mace
- ½ teaspoon salt
- Honey Nut Topping
- Whipped cream, optional

In a large bowl, cream sugar and butter. Add eggs, one at a time, beating after each addition. Beat in honey; set aside. In a small bowl, combine milk and almond flavoring; set aside. In another bowl, sift together flour, baking powder, mace, and salt; add to creamed mixture alternately with milk, beating well after each addition. Pour batter into two greased and floured 8-inch round cake pans. Bake in a preheated 350° F. oven 35 minutes. Spread layers with Honey Nut Topping and bake about 5 minutes longer. Cool; remove from pans. Stack layers and frost with whipped cream, if desired.

Honey Nut Topping

- ⅓ cup honey
- ½ cup chopped nuts
- ¼ cup brown sugar
- ½ teaspoon cinnamon
- ¼ cup softened butter

Mix together all ingredients and spread on hot layers.

Quick Orange Coffee Cake
Makes 1 coffee cake

- ⅔ cup sugar
- 1 tablespoon grated orange peel
- 2 packages (10 ounces each) refrigerated buttermilk biscuits
- 3 tablespoons butter *or* margarine, melted
- ½ cup powdered sugar
- 1 tablespoon orange juice

In a small bowl, mix together sugar and orange peel; set aside. Separate biscuits. Dip each into melted butter, then into sugar mixture to coat well. In a greased 9-inch round baking pan, arrange dough to overlap slightly. Sprinkle any remaining sugar mixture on top. Bake in a preheated 375° F. oven 35 minutes or until golden brown. Cool on a wire rack 10 minutes. Turn out onto a serving plate. In a small bowl, combine powdered sugar and orange juice; blend well. Drizzle over coffee cake.

Cakes & Pies

Blueberry Coffee Cake
Makes 1 coffee cake

- 1 egg, lightly beaten
- 10 tablespoons sugar, divided
- 1¼ cups flour
- 2 teaspoons baking powder
- ¾ teaspoon salt
- ½ cup milk
- 3 tablespoons butter *or* margarine, melted
- 1 cup fresh blueberries
- 1 tablespoon butter *or* margarine, melted

In a mixing bowl, blend egg and 8 tablespoons sugar. In a separate bowl, sift together flour, baking powder, and salt. Alternately add flour and milk to egg mixture; beat well after each addition. Stir in 3 tablespoons melted butter. Fold in blueberries. Turn batter into a greased 8-inch square baking pan. Sprinkle with remaining 2 tablespoons sugar. Cover and refrigerate overnight. Preheat oven to 350° F. Bake 35 minutes or until top springs back when lightly touched. Brush top with remaining butter. Cool in pan on a wire rack.

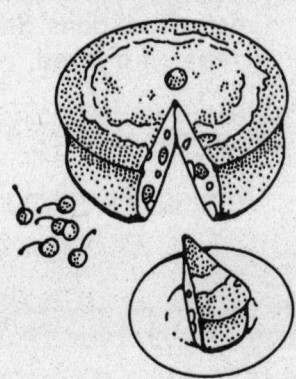

Old-Fashioned Pound Cake
Makes one 10-inch tube cake

- 2 cups butter *or* margarine
- 3½ cups sugar
- 10 eggs
- 4 cups flour
- 1 teaspoon vanilla
- Lemon Glaze

In a large mixing bowl, cream butter and sugar until light and fluffy. Add eggs, one at a time, beating well after each addition. Gradually add flour; blend well. Pour batter into a greased 10-inch tube pan. Bake in a preheated 300° F. oven 2 hours or until a wooden pick inserted near the center comes out clean. Cool in pan 10 minutes before turning out onto a wire rack to cool completely. Drizzle Lemon Glaze over the top.

Lemon Glaze

- 2 tablespoons butter *or* margarine
- 4 teaspoons lemon juice
- 1 cup sifted powdered sugar

In a small bowl, combine sugar, lemon juice, and butter; blend until smooth. Let glaze stand for 3 to 4 minutes to thicken.

Cakes & Pies

Frosty Spice Cake
Makes one 8-inch cake

- ½ cup shortening
- 1 cup sugar
- 2 eggs
- 2¼ cups sifted cake flour
- 2 teaspoons cinnamon
- 1 teaspoon baking powder
- 1 teaspoon cloves
- ½ teaspoon baking soda
- 1 teaspoon salt
- ¼ teaspoon nutmeg
- ⅛ teaspoon allspice
- 1 cup dairy sour cream
- Frosty Icing
- ⅓ cup chopped walnuts

In a large bowl, cream shortening and sugar. Add eggs, one at a time, beating well after each; set aside. In another bowl, sift together dry ingredients; add to creamed mixture alternately with sour cream. Pour into two greased 8-inch cake pans. Bake in a preheated 375° F. oven 25 to 30 minutes. Cool; frost with Frosty Icing. Sprinkle with walnuts.

Frosty Icing

- 1 cup packed light brown sugar
- 2 egg whites
- 3 tablespoons cold water
- ½ teaspoon vanilla

In the top of a double boiler, mix sugar, egg whites, and water. Place over boiling water. Beat constantly with electric mixer until stiff peaks form, 4 to 5 minutes. Remove top pan from heat. Add vanilla; beat 1 minute longer. Spread on cake immediately.

Cakes & Pies

Carrot Cake with Pineapple
Makes one 10-inch tube cake

- 2 cups sugar
- 1⅓ cups vegetable oil
- 3 eggs, beaten
- 3 cups flour
- 2 teaspoons baking soda
- 2 teaspoons cinnamon
- 1 teaspoon salt
- 2 cups grated carrots
- 1 cup chopped walnuts or pecans
- 1 cup drained crushed pineapple
- 2 teaspoons vanilla
- Lemon Glaze

In a small bowl, blend sugar, oil, and eggs; set aside. In a large bowl, sift together flour, soda, cinnamon, and salt. Make a hollow in the dry mixture and pour in the sugar mixture; mix well. Add the carrots, nuts, pineapple and vanilla. Pour the batter into an ungreased 10-inch tube pan, and bake in a preheated 350° F. oven for an hour and 15 minutes. Cool cake in pan 15 minutes; loosen sides and remove from pan. Ice with Lemon Glaze.

Lemon Glaze

- 1 cup powdered sugar, sifted
- 2 tablespoons lemon juice
- 3 tablespoons butter, melted

In a small bowl, combine sugar, lemon juice, and butter; blend until smooth. Let glaze stand for 3 to 4 minutes to thicken.

Plum Crazy Cake
Makes one 9-inch cake

- 3 cups pitted and quartered plums
- 1⅔ cups sugar, divided
- 2 tablespoons cornstarch
- 1 teaspoon orange peel
- ½ cup orange juice
- ½ cup water
- ¼ cup butter
- 1 egg
- 2 cups sifted all-purpose flour
- 1 tablespoon baking powder
- ¼ teaspoon salt
- 1 cup milk
- Sweetened whipped cream

Arrange plums, skin side down, in a 9-inch square baking pan. In a 2-quart saucepan, mix 1 cup sugar and cornstarch; gradually add orange peel, juice, and water. Cook over medium heat, stirring until thickened. Cook 2 additional minutes. Pour over plums. In a bowl, cream butter and remaining sugar. Beat in egg; set aside. In another bowl, sift together flour, baking powder, and salt; add to creamed mixture alternately with milk. Carefully spoon mixture over top of plums; spread evenly to cover orange mixture. Bake in preheated 350° F. oven 45 minutes. Cool in pan on wire rack 5 minutes. Invert onto serving plate so that plums are on the top. Serve with whipped cream.

Cakes & Pies

Glazed Williamsburg Pound Cake
Makes one 10-inch tube cake

- 2 cups butter, softened
- 3 cups sugar
- 12 egg yolks, well beaten
- 12 egg whites, beaten to stiff peaks
- 4 cups all-purpose flour, sifted
- Cranberry Glaze
- Whole cranberries, optional

In a bowl, cream butter and sugar. Alternately add egg yolks, egg whites, and flour to butter mixture. Beat until light and smooth. Pour into greased and floured 10-inch tube pan. Bake in preheated 325° F. oven about 1½ hours or until golden brown. Cool in pan 30 minutes before removing. Drizzle cooled Cranberry Glaze over cake. Decorate with whole cranberries, if desired.

Cranberry Glaze

- 2 cups water
- 2 cups sugar
- 1 pound (4 cups) cranberries

In a saucepan, bring water and sugar to rapid boil. Simmer 10 minutes. Add cranberries. Cook until cranberries pop, about 5 minutes. Remove cranberries with slotted spoon to a small bowl (store in refrigerator for another use). Continue to cook syrup until thickened, about 20 minutes. Cool before using.

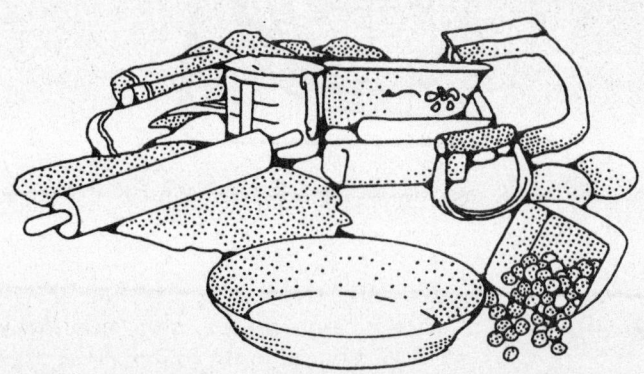

Piecrust*
Makes 2 piecrusts or 1 double crust pie

- 1 cup vegetable shortening
- 3 cups sifted flour
- 1½ teaspoon salt
- ½ cup ice water

In a mixing bowl, cut shortening into flour and salt using a pastry blender or two knives until consistency of small peas. Blend in water, 1 tablespoon at a time, tossing with a fork. Gather dough into a ball.

*This recipe can be used for all pies in this chapter calling for piecrust.

Cakes & Pies

Plum Pie
Makes 1 pie

Pastry for 9-inch double piecrust
4 cups sliced plums
1 tablespoon lemon juice
½ teaspoon almond extract
¼ cup butter *or* margarine
¼ cup flour
1½ cups sugar

Roll half of pastry and line a 9-inch pie pan; set aside. Gently toss plums with lemon juice and almond extract; place in pie shell. Dot with butter. In a small bowl, combine flour and sugar; sprinkle over fruit. Roll remaining pastry to fit over pie; seal edges. Cut slits in top to vent steam. Bake in a preheated 450° F. oven 35 to 45 minutes until brown and bubbly. Cool on rack.

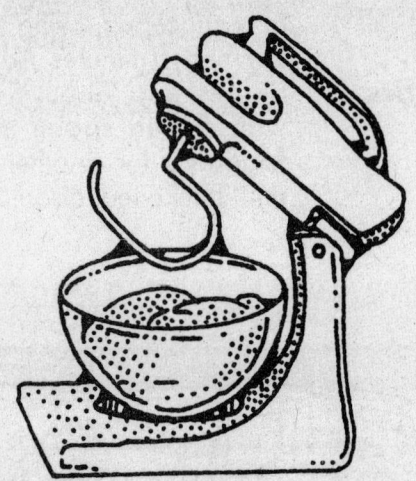

Sweet Potato Pie
Makes 1 pie

3 cups cooked sweet potatoes, pureed
1 cup firmly packed light brown sugar
½ teaspoon cinnamon
¼ teaspoon each allspice, nutmeg, and salt
3 eggs, beaten
½ pint half-and-half
4 tablespoons melted butter
1 unbaked 9-inch pie shell

In a bowl, mix all ingredients except pie shell. Mound into unbaked pie shell; smooth surface with a spatula. Bake in a preheated 450° F. oven 10 minutes; reduce heat to 250° F. and continue baking for 20 minutes or until wooden pick inserted in center comes out clean. Serve hot or cold.

Cakes & Pies

Pink Ribbon Apple Pie
Makes 1 pie

- 8 to 9 tart apples, sliced
- ¼ cup lemon juice
- Piecrust
- 1½ to 2 cups sugar
- 3 tablespoons flour
- 1 teaspoon salt
- 1 teaspoon ground cinnamon
- ½ teaspoon ground nutmeg
- Butter

Slice apples; place in a bowl of ice water with lemon juice. Prepare piecrust. Divide dough. Roll out one half on a floured pastry cloth 1 inch larger than a 9-inch pie plate. Fit dough into pie plate. Drain apples on paper towels. Place a layer of apples in prepared pie plate. In a small bowl, combine sugar, flour, salt, cinnamon, and nutmeg; blend well. Sprinkle some of the sugar mixture over apple layer; dot with butter. Repeat layers until all apples are used, ending with sugar mixture and butter. Roll out remaining dough. Place on top of apples. Press top and bottom crusts together; trim and flute edge. Cut slits in the top to vent steam. Bake on middle rack in oven at 400° F. 10 minutes. Reduce heat to 350° F. and bake 40 minutes or until bubbly and golden.

Lemon Lattice Pie
Makes 1 pie

- 2 cups sugar
- ¼ cup plus 2 tablespoons flour
- 6 eggs, beaten
- ½ cup butter
- 1 cup lemon juice
- 2 teaspoons grated lemon peel
- 1 9-inch unbaked pastry shell
- Lattice

Mix sugar and flour in top of double boiler; beat in eggs, butter, lemon juice and lemon peel. Cook, stirring constantly, 12 to 15 minutes or until mixture thickens. Cool. Pour into pie shell; set aside. Prepare Lattice; weave into lattice design on top of custard-filled pie shell. Preheat oven to 350°. Bake 30 to 35 minutes until golden brown. Cool on rack.

Lattice

- 1 cup flour
- ½ cup light brown sugar, packed
- 1 teaspoon baking powder
- ¼ teaspoon ground nutmeg
- ¼ cup butter *or* margarine
- 1 egg, lightly beaten
- 1 tablespoon milk

Mix flour, sugar, baking powder, and nutmeg in bowl; cut in butter until mixture resembles small peas. Stir in egg and milk. Knead slightly; form into ball. Chill 30 minutes. Roll dough into 11-inch circle on lightly floured surface; cut into strips.

Cakes & Pies

Pecan Pie
Makes 1 pie

- 3 eggs
- ½ cup sugar
- 1 cup dark corn syrup
- ⅛ teaspoon salt
- 1 teaspoon vanilla
- ¼ cup butter *or* margarine, melted
- 1 cup whole pecans
- 1 unbaked 9-inch pastry shell

Beat eggs in a bowl; add sugar and syrup. Beat in salt, vanilla, and butter; set aside. Spread pecans evenly in bottom of pie shell; add filling. Bake in a preheated 350° F. oven 50 to 60 minutes. Nuts will rise to top of pie to form crust. Cool on rack.

Deep Dish Strawberry-Rhubarb Pie
Makes 1 pie

- 3 cups ½-inch rhubarb pieces
- 2 cups sliced strawberries
- 1 tablespoon lemon juice
- 1½ cups sugar
- 3 tablespoons tapioca
- ½ teaspoon vanilla
- 2 tablespoons butter *or* margarine
- Pastry for 9-inch single piecrust
- 1 tablespoon sugar

Place fruits and lemon juice in an 8-inch square baking dish. Combine 1½ cups sugar and tapioca; toss gently with fruit. Sprinkle with vanilla and dot with butter. Roll pastry to 9-inch square and place over fruit. Crimp at edge of pan to seal; cut 3 slits to vent steam. Sprinkle with 1 tablespoon sugar. Bake in a preheated 400° F. oven 45 to 50 minutes until crust is golden brown. Cool on rack.

Cakes & Pies

Fresh Cherry Pie
Makes 1 pie

Pastry for 9-inch double piecrust
- 1⅓ cups sugar
- ⅓ cup flour
- ⅛ teaspoon salt
- 4 cups pitted tart cherries
- 3 drops almond extract, optional
- 2 tablespoons butter *or* margarine

Divide piecrust dough in half. Roll out half and fit into a 9-inch pie plate; set aside. In a small bowl, combine sugar, flour, and salt; set aside. In a separate bowl, combine cherries and almond extract. Sprinkle with flour mixture; toss lightly to mix. Turn cherry mixture into prepared crust. Dot with butter. Roll out remaining dough. Cut into ½-inch strips. Weave strips into a lattice top. Trim, seal, and flute edge. Bake in a preheated 425° F. oven 40 minutes or until bubbly.

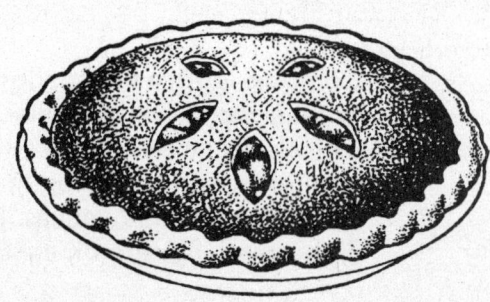

Sour Cream Pumpkin Pie
Makes 1 pie

- 1 cup firmly packed light brown sugar
- 1 tablespoon flour
- ½ teaspoon salt
- 1 teaspoon ground ginger
- ½ teaspoon ground nutmeg
- ½ teaspoon ground cloves
- ½ teaspoon ground cinnamon
- 1 cup canned pumpkin
- 2 eggs, well beaten
- 1 cup evaporated milk
- ½ cup dairy sour cream
- ½ cup chopped walnuts
- 1 unbaked 9-inch pastry shell
- Whipped cream, optional

In a bowl mix brown sugar, flour, salt, and spices. Add pumpkin, eggs, milk, sour cream, and walnuts; mix well. Pour into crust. Bake in a preheated 400° F. oven 40 to 50 minutes or until knife inserted in center comes out clean. Cool on rack. Edge crust with whipped cream, if desired.

Cakes & Pies

Almond Chiffon Cake
Makes one 10-inch tube cake

- 2 cups sifted all-purpose flour
- 1½ cups sugar
- 1 tablespoon baking powder
- 1 teaspoon salt
- 7 eggs, separated
- ½ cup vegetable oil
- 1 teaspoon lemon extract
- 1 teaspoon almond extract
- ¾ cup ice water
- ½ teaspoon cream of tartar
- Double Boiler Frosting
- Sliced almonds

In a bowl, sift first 4 ingredients together four times; set aside. In another bowl, combine egg yolks, vegetable oil, extracts, and ice water. Add dry ingredients; mix well and set aside. Beat egg whites and cream of tartar until stiff peaks form. Gradually fold egg whites into flour mixture. Pour into ungreased 10-inch tube pan. Bake in a preheated 325° F. oven for 55 minutes; increase temperature to 350° F. and bake 10 minutes longer. Invert to cool for 1½ to 2 hours. Ice with Double Boiler Frosting, and sprinkle sliced almonds on top.

Double Boiler Frosting

- 2 egg whites
- 1½ cups sugar
- ¼ teaspoon cream of tartar
- ⅓ cup water
- 1 teaspoon vanilla

Combine egg whites, sugar, cream of tartar, and water in top of double boiler. Beat on high for 1 minute with electric mixer. Place over boiling water and beat on high speed for seven minutes. Remove pan from boiling water. Add vanilla. Beat 2 minutes longer on high speed. Spread on cake.

Potato Cake
Makes one 9 x 13-inch cake

- 1 cup butter *or* **margarine,** softened
- 2 cups sugar
- 4 eggs, separated
- 1 cup unseasoned mashed potatoes
- 1 cup chopped nuts
- 1 teaspoon ground cinnamon
- 1 teaspoon ground cloves
- 1 teaspoon ground nutmeg
- 2½ cups flour
- 2 teaspoons baking powder
- ½ cup milk

In a large mixing bowl, cream butter and sugar with an electric mixer until light and fluffy. Add egg yolks, potatoes, nuts, and spices; blend well. In a separate bowl, combine flour and baking powder. Alternately add flour mixture and milk to creamed mixture; blend well. In a small bowl, beat egg whites with electric mixer until stiff peaks form. Gently fold egg whites into batter. Pour batter into a greased and floured 9 x 13-inch baking pan. Bake in a preheated 350° F. oven 45 minutes or until a toothpick inserted in the center comes out clean.

Cookies

Thumbprint Cookies
Makes about 3 dozen

- 1 cup granulated sugar
- 1 cup brown sugar
- 1¼ cups margarine
- 3 eggs
- 2 teaspoons vanilla
- 4 cups sifted flour
- 1 teaspoon salt
- 1 teaspoon baking soda
- 1 teaspoon baking powder
- 1 teaspoon cinnamon
- 1 cup chopped dates, optional
- 1 cup chopped nuts, optional
- ¼ cup warm water
- Orange marmalade *or* strawberry preserves

Cream sugars and margarine. Add eggs and vanilla and beat well; set aside. In a large bowl, sift together flour, salt, baking soda, baking powder, and cinnamon. Add dry ingredients to creamed mixture. Mix in dates and nuts, if desired. Add the warm water. Drop by tablespoons onto ungreased cookie sheet. Make a thumbprint in the center of each cookie, and fill indentations with marmalade or strawberry preserves. Bake in a preheated 375° F. oven for 12 minutes.

Cookies

Cherry Thumbprints
Makes about 3½ dozen

- 1½ cups all-purpose flour
- ¼ cup sugar
- ½ cup butter, softened
- 1 egg
- 1 teaspoon vanilla
- ¼ teaspoon salt
- ¼ cup finely chopped nuts
- 1 teaspoon grated lemon peel
- Powdered sugar
- Cherry Filling

In a large mixing bowl, combine flour, sugar, butter, egg, vanilla, and salt; blend well. Stir in nuts and lemon peel. Gently shape dough into 1-inch balls. Place on an ungreased baking sheet. Press thumb deeply into center of each ball. Bake at 350° F. for 10 minutes or until cookies are set. Remove from baking sheet to a wire rack to cool. Roll cookies in powdered sugar. Prepare Cherry Filling. Spoon one cherry into the center of each cookie. For best results, fill cookies on the day they are to be served.

Cherry Filling

- 1 can (16 or 17 ounces) pitted dark sweet cherries, drained; reserve ⅓ cup juice
- 2 teaspoons cornstarch
- Dash salt

In a saucepan, combine reserved cherry juice and cornstarch. Add salt. Cook over medium heat, stirring constantly until thickened and clear. Stir in the cherries. Let stand until cool.

Molasses Cookies
Makes about 6 dozen cookies

- 1 pound brown sugar
- 2 cups molasses
- 1 cup shortening
- 2 teaspoons ginger
- 2 teaspoons cinnamon
- 1 teaspoon salt
- 1 teaspoon baking soda
- ½ teaspoon cloves
- ½ cup boiling water
- 2 pounds flour

Mix brown sugar, molasses, and shortening together in large bowl. Add spices; blend well. Mix in boiling water. Gradually blend in flour, making a stiff dough. Roll out very thin, cut with cookie cutters, and place on greased cookie sheets. Bake in a preheated 350° F. oven 8 minutes. Cool and store.

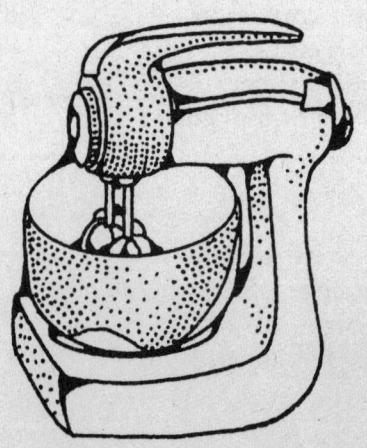

Cookies

Walnut Crescents
Makes about 5 dozen

- 1 cup butter, softened
- ¾ cup sugar
- 1½ teaspoons vanilla
- 2½ cups all-purpose flour
- 1 cup finely chopped walnuts
- Chocolate Glaze
- Chocolate jimmies *or* flaked coconut

In a large mixing bowl, cream butter and sugar until smooth. Add vanilla; blend well. Gradually blend in flour; stir in nuts. Shape spoonfuls of dough into rolls about 3 inches long. Place on an ungreased baking sheet. Pull ends down to form a crescent. Bake at 350° F. for 15 to 16 minutes or until golden. Cool slightly on pan. Remove to wire rack to cool completely. Dip ends in Chocolate Glaze, then in jimmies or coconut.

Chocolate Glaze

- 1½ ounces semisweet baking chocolate
- 1½ teaspoons light corn syrup
- 1½ teaspoons cream

In a small saucepan, combine all ingredients. Cook over low heat, stirring constantly until smooth.

Applesauce Cookies
Makes 5 dozen

- 1¾ cups all-purpose flour
- ½ teaspoon baking powder
- 1 teaspoon baking soda
- ¼ teaspoon salt
- 1 teaspoon cinnamon
- ½ teaspoon cloves
- ½ teaspoon nutmeg
- ¾ cup butter *or* margarine, softened
- 1 cup sugar
- 1 egg
- 1 cup thick sweetened applesauce
- ½ cup raisins
- 1 cup cornflakes, crushed

Combine flour, baking powder, baking soda, salt, and spices; set aside. In a large mixing bowl, cream butter and sugar until smooth. Blend in egg. Add dry ingredients alternately with applesauce to creamed mixture, beating after each addition. Stir in raisins and cereal. Drop batter by teaspoonfuls about 2 inches apart onto a greased and floured baking sheet. Bake at 375° F. for 10 minutes or until golden. Remove from baking sheet to a wire rack to cool.

Cookies

Date-Nut Roll Cookies
Makes about 3 dozen

- 2 cups brown sugar
- 1 cup shortening
- 3 eggs, well beaten
- 4 cups enriched flour
- ½ teaspoon salt
- ½ teaspoon soda

In a large bowl, cream sugar, shortening, and eggs; set aside. In another bowl, sift together flour, salt, and soda. Blend into creamed mixture and mix well. Divide dough into 4 parts; roll each out to ¼-inch thickness, and spread filling over all. Roll up each part, wrap in wax paper, and chill in refrigerator several hours. Cut in ¼-inch slices and bake on an ungreased cookie sheet in a preheated 375° F. oven for 12 minutes.

Filling

- 2 packages (8 ounces) dates, chopped
- 1 cup sugar
- 1 cup water
- 1 cup chopped pecans
- ¼ cup chopped candied cherries
- ¼ cup chopped candied pineapple

In a saucepan, cook dates, sugar, and water over low heat for 10 minutes. Stir in nuts, cherries, and pineapple; let cool.

Pinwheels
Makes about 7 dozen

- ¾ cup vegetable shortening *or* butter/shortening mixture
- 1 cup sugar
- 2 eggs
- 1 teaspoon vanilla
- 2½ cups all-purpose flour
- 1 teaspoon baking powder
- 1 teaspoon salt
- 2 squares (1 ounce each) unsweetened baking chocolate, melted and cooled

In a large mixing bowl, cream shortening and sugar until smooth. Blend in eggs and vanilla. Stir together flour, baking powder, and salt. Gradually add dry ingredients to creamed mixture; blend well. Divide dough in half. Blend chocolate into one half. Cover and chill both doughs until firm. Roll each dough into a 12 x 9-inch rectangle. Place chocolate dough on top of plain dough. Roll to about ¼ inch thick. Roll up from the long side. Wrap in plastic wrap and chill until firm. Cut into ⅛-inch slices. Place on an ungreased baking sheet. Bake at 400° F. for 8 to 10 minutes or until set. Remove from baking sheet to a wire rack to cool.

Cookies

Pink Party Sandwiches
Makes about 4 dozen

- 1¼ cups butter, softened
- 2 cups sugar
- 2 eggs
- 1 teaspoon vanilla
- 1½ cups sifted all-purpose flour
- 1½ cups cornstarch
- ½ teaspoon cream of tartar
- Pink Butter Filling

In a large mixing bowl, cream butter and sugar until smooth. Blend in eggs and vanilla. Stir together flour, cornstarch, and cream of tartar. Gradually add flour mixture to creamed mixture; blend well. Chill dough until firm. Roll out dough on a lightly floured surface to ⅛-inch thickness. Cut out with a floured 3-inch cookie cutter. Place on a greased baking sheet. Bake at 400° F. for about 8 minutes or until edges are golden brown. Remove from baking sheet to a wire rack to cool. Fill cookies with Pink Butter Filling.

Pink Butter Filling

- ¼ cup butter, softened
- 2 cups sifted powdered sugar
- ¼ cup whipping cream
- 1 teaspoon vanilla
- Red food coloring

Cream butter until light and fluffy. Gradually beat in sugar, cream, and vanilla. Tint with red food coloring. Beat until filling is of spreading consistency.

Cookies

Sugar Cookies
Makes 6 dozen

- 1 cup granulated sugar
- 1 cup powdered sugar
- 1 cup butter *or* margarine, softened
- 1 cup vegetable oil
- 2 eggs
- 1 teaspoon baking soda
- 1 teaspoon cream of tartar
- ½ teaspoon salt
- 1 teaspoon vanilla
- 4½ cups flour
- Granulated sugar

In a large mixing bowl, combine sugars, butter, oil, and eggs; beat until well blended. Beat in baking soda, cream of tartar, salt, and vanilla. Gradually add flour; beat until well blended. Cover and chill well. Roll dough into 1-inch balls. Roll balls in granulated sugar. Place balls 2 inches apart on a baking sheet. Flatten with the bottom of a glass. Bake at 375° F. 10 to 12 minutes. Cool on a wire rack.

Cranberry Charms
Makes about 6 dozen

- 2 cups fresh cranberries, coarsely chopped
- 1 cup granulated sugar, divided
- 1 cup vegetable shortening
- 1¼ cups packed light brown sugar
- 2 eggs
- 1¾ cups all-purpose flour
- 1 teaspoon salt
- 1 teaspoon baking powder
- 1 teaspoon baking soda
- 1 teaspoon cinnamon
- 1 teaspoon nutmeg
- ½ cup buttermilk *or* sour milk*
- 1 teaspoon vanilla
- 1 tablespoon grated orange peel
- 3 cups rolled oats
- 1 cup chopped nuts

In a small bowl, combine cranberries and ¾ cup granulated sugar; set aside for 30 minutes. In a large mixing bowl, cream remaining ¼ cup granulated sugar, shortening, brown sugar, and eggs until blended. Stir together flour, salt, baking powder, baking soda, and spices. Add dry ingredients alternately with buttermilk and vanilla to creamed mixture, beating well after each addition. Stir in orange peel, oats, nuts, and 1 cup of the cranberry-sugar mixture. Drop batter by tablespoonfuls 2 inches apart onto a greased baking sheet. Top cookies with remaining chopped cranberries. Bake at 400° F. for 10 minutes or until cookies are brown around the edges.

*To sour milk, mix 1½ teaspoons lemon juice into milk to equal ½ cup.

Cookies

Dark Chocolate Drop Cookies
Makes 4½ dozen

- ½ cup butter *or* margarine, softened
- 1 cup packed brown sugar
- 1 egg
- 1 teaspoon vanilla
- 2 squares (1 ounce each) unsweetened baking chocolate, melted and cooled
- 2 cups all-purpose flour
- ½ teaspoon baking soda
- ¼ teaspoon salt
- ¾ cup dairy sour cream
- ½ cup chopped pecans
- Mocha Frosting

In a large mixing bowl, cream butter and brown sugar until smooth. Blend in egg, vanilla, and chocolate. Stir together flour, baking soda, and salt. Add dry ingredients alternately with sour cream to chocolate mixture, beating well after each addition. Stir in pecans. Drop batter by teaspoonfuls 2 inches apart onto a greased and floured baking sheet. Bake at 350° F. for 10 minutes or until set. Remove from baking sheet to a wire rack to cool. Frost with Mocha Frosting.

Mocha Frosting

- ¼ cup butter, softened
- 2 tablespoons unsweetened cocoa
- 2 teaspoons instant coffee granules
- ¼ teaspoon salt
- 3 cups powdered sugar
- 3 tablespoons milk
- 1½ teaspooons vanilla

In a medium mixing bowl, cream butter, cocoa, instant coffee, and salt until smooth. Gradually add powdered sugar, milk, and vanilla. Beat until frosting is smooth and of spreading consistency.

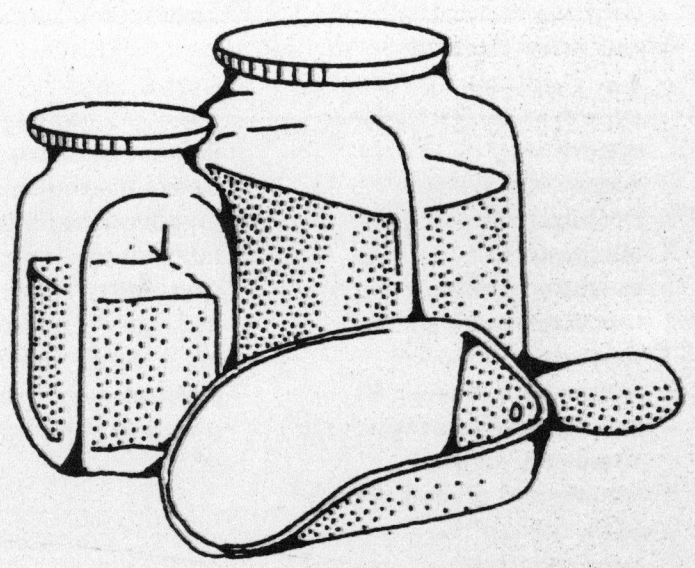

Cookies

Golden Apple Cookies
Makes about 3½ dozen

- 1 cup vegetable shortening
- ¾ cup granulated sugar
- ¾ cup packed brown sugar
- 3 eggs
- 1 tablespoon grated orange peel
- 2 cups all-purpose flour
- 2 teaspoons baking powder
- 1 teaspoon cinnamon
- ½ teaspoon cloves
- ½ teaspoon nutmeg
- ½ teaspoon salt
- 3 or 4 Golden Delicious apples
- 2 cups rolled oats
- ½ cup raisins
- ½ cup chopped nuts

In a large mixing bowl, cream shortening and sugars until smooth. Blend in eggs and orange peel. Combine flour, baking powder, spices, and salt. Gradually add dry ingredients to creamed mixture; blend well. Pare, core, and chop apples to equal 3 cups. Stir in apples, oats, raisins, and nuts. Drop batter by rounded tablespoonfuls 2 inches apart onto a greased baking sheet. Bake at 350° F. for 15 to 17 minutes or until lightly browned. Remove from baking sheet to a wire rack to cool.

Chocolate Acorns
Makes 5 dozen

- 3 egg whites
- 1 tablespoon vinegar
- ¼ teaspoon salt
- 1 cup sugar
- 1 teaspoon vanilla
- ½ pound ground blanched almonds
- 4 squares (1 ounce each) unsweetened baking chocolate, melted
- 1 cup semisweet chocolate chips, melted
- ½ cup finely chopped pistachio nuts

In a large mixing bowl, beat egg whites until soft peaks form. Add vinegar and salt; continue beating. Gradually add sugar, beating until stiff peaks form. Fold in vanilla, almonds, and melted unsweetened chocolate. Drop batter by rounded teaspoonfuls 1 inch apart onto a greased baking sheet. Bake at 250° for 25 to 30 minutes or until set. Remove from baking sheet to a wire rack to cool. Dip half of each cookie into the melted chocolate chips; sprinkle with pistachios.

Cookies

Pecan Butter Balls
Makes about 3 dozen

- 1 cup butter, softened
- ½ cup powdered sugar
- ½ teaspoon vanilla
- 1¾ cups all-purpose flour
- ½ cup chopped pecans

In a large mixing bowl, cream butter and sugar until light and fluffy. Blend in vanilla. Gradually add flour; blend well. Stir in nuts. Cover and chill until firm. Shape dough into 1-inch balls. Place on a greased baking sheet. Bake at 350° F. for 20 minutes or until golden brown. Remove from baking sheet to a wire rack to cool.

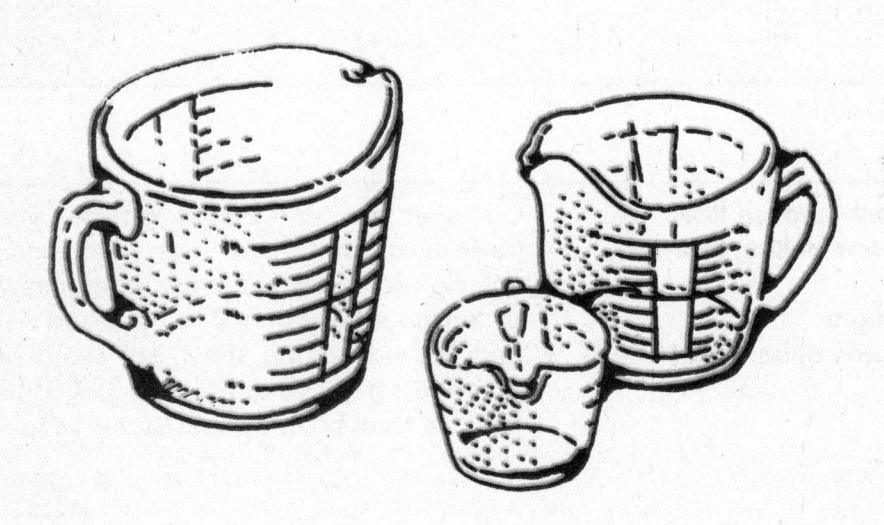

Drop Sugar Cookies
Makes about 5 dozen

- ⅔ cup vegetable shortening
- 1⅔ cups sugar
- 2 eggs
- 2 teaspoons vanilla
- 3½ cups sifted all-purpose flour
- ½ teaspoon baking soda
- 1 teaspoon salt
- 2 teaspoons baking powder
- ½ cup dairy sour cream

In a large mixing bowl, cream shortening and sugar until smooth. Add eggs and vanilla; blend well. In another bowl, stir together flour, baking soda, salt, and baking powder. Add dry ingredients alternately with sour cream to creamed mixture, beating well after each addition. Drop batter by teaspoonfuls 2 inches apart onto an ungreased baking sheet. Bake at 375° F. for 12 minutes or until just golden. Remove from baking sheet to a wire rack to cool.

Cookies

Anise Drops
Makes 4 dozen

1½ cups all-purpose flour
¼ teaspoon baking powder
2 eggs
1 cup sugar
¼ teaspoon anise extract

Combine flour and baking powder; set aside. In a large mixing bowl, beat eggs, sugar, and anise extract until light-colored. Stir in dry ingredients. Drop batter by teaspoonfuls about 2 inches apart onto a greased and floured baking sheet. Let stand at room temperature for 6 hours. Bake at 350° F. for 6 minutes. Remove from baking sheet to a wire rack to cool.

Bear Paw Cookies
Makes about 3 dozen

1 cup butter *or* margarine, softened
⅔ cup sugar
½ cup chocolate-flavored syrup
2 eggs
1 teaspoon vanilla
2⅓ cups all-purpose flour
2 teaspoons baking powder
1 teaspoon salt
¼ cup milk
Peanut halves *or* cashews

In a large mixing bowl, cream butter and sugar until light and fluffy. Blend in chocolate syrup. Add eggs, 1 at a time, beating well after each addition. Blend in vanilla. Combine flour, baking powder, and salt. Add dry ingredients alternately with milk to chocolate mixture, beating well after each addition. Cover and chill 1 hour. Drop batter by heaping teaspoonfuls onto a greased baking sheet. Press 4 peanut halves into each cookie. Bake at 375° F. for 10 to 12 minutes or until centers spring back when light touched. Cool on the baking sheet 2 minutes; transfer to a wire rack to cool completely.

Cookies

Almond Slices
Makes about 7 dozen

- 1½ cups sliced unblanched almonds
- 2 cups all-purpose flour
- 1 cup sugar
- 1 teaspoon ground cinnamon
- 1 cup butter, softened
- 2 eggs

In a large mixing bowl, combine almonds, flour, sugar, and cinnamon. Add butter and eggs; blend well. Divide dough in half. Shape dough into 2 long blocks 3 inches wide. Wrap in plastic wrap and chill overnight. Cut dough into ⅛-inch slices. Place about 1 inch apart on a baking sheet. Bake at 375° F. for 10 minutes or until edges are lightly browned. Remove from baking sheet to a wire rack to cool.

Snow-Covered Gingersnaps
Makes about 3 dozen

- ¾ cup shortening
- 1 cup granulated sugar
- 4 tablespoons molasses
- 1 egg
- 2 cups unsifted all-purpose flour
- 2 teaspoons baking soda
- 1 teaspoon salt
- 1 teaspoon cloves
- 1 teaspoon cinnamon
- 1 teaspoon ginger
- Powdered sugar

In a large bowl, cream shortening and sugar. Add molasses and egg, beating well after each addition; set aside. In another bowl, sift together flour, baking soda, salt, and spices. Add to creamed mixture to form dough. Roll into balls the size of a walnut. Roll balls in powdered sugar. Place on ungreased cookie sheet. Bake in a preheated 350° F. oven for 10 to 12 minutes. Sprinkle with powdered sugar before removing from cookie sheet.

Cookies

Currant Cakes
Makes 3 dozen

- 1 cup butter, softened
- 1 teaspoon grated lemon peel
- 1 tablespoon lemon juice
- 1 cup sugar
- 3 eggs, well beaten
- 1¾ cups all-purpose flour
- ¼ teaspoon salt
- ¾ cup dried currants

In a large mixing bowl, cream butter, lemon peel, and lemon juice until light. Add sugar; cream until light and fluffy. Add eggs; blend well. In another bowl, mix flour and salt; gradually add to creamed mixture, beating until well blended. Stir in currants. Drop batter by teaspoonfuls onto a greased and floured baking sheet. Bake at 350° F. for 10 minutes or until set. Remove from baking sheet to a wire rack to cool.

Fruit Swirls
Makes about 3 dozen

- ¾ cup vegetable shortening
- ¾ cup granulated sugar
- ¾ packed brown sugar
- 1 egg
- 1 teaspoon vanilla
- 2 cups flour
- 1½ teaspoons baking powder
- ¾ teaspoon salt
- ½ cup raspberry preserves

In a large mixing bowl, cream shortening and sugars until smooth. Add egg and vanilla; blend well. Stir together flour, baking powder, and salt. Gradually add to creamed mixture; blend until smooth. Stir in raspberry preserves until just blended. Do not overblend. Drop batter by teaspoonfuls about 2 inches apart onto an ungreased baking sheet. Bake at 375° F. for 12 to 15 minutes or until lightly browned. Remove from baking sheet to a wire rack to cool.

Cookies

Brown Sugar Icebox Cookies
Makes about 5 dozen

- 1 cup packed dark brown sugar
- 1 cup granulated sugar
- 3 eggs
- 1½ cups vegetable shortening
- 4½ cups all-purpose flour
- 2 teaspoons baking soda
- ¼ teaspoon salt
- 1 teaspoon ground cinnamon
- 1 cup chopped pecans

In a large mixing bowl, combine sugars, eggs, and shortening; cream until light and fluffy. Stir together flour, baking soda, salt, and cinnamon. Gradually add dry ingredients to creamed mixture; blend well. Stir in pecans. Divide doughs into thirds. Shape each third into 1½-inch wide log. Wrap in plastic wrap and chill overnight. Cut dough into ⅛-inch slices. Place on a greased and floured baking sheet. Bake at 375° F. for 8 minutes. Watch carefully: these cookies burn easily. Remove from baking sheet to a wire rack to cool.

Vermont Drop Cookies
Makes 8 dozen

- ¾ cup maple syrup
- ¾ cup packed dark brown sugar
- 4 eggs
- ¾ cup vegetable oil
- 1 teaspoon vanilla
- 1 cup skim milk powder
- 2¾ cups quick-cooking rolled oats
- 1 cup wheat germ
- 1 cup golden raisins

In a large mixing bowl, combine maple syrup, brown sugar, eggs, oil, and vanilla; blend well. Stir in remaining ingredients in order given. Drop batter by teaspoonfuls onto a greased baking sheet. Bake at 350° F. for 12 to 15 minutes or until set. Remove from baking sheet to a wire rack to cool. Store in refrigerator.

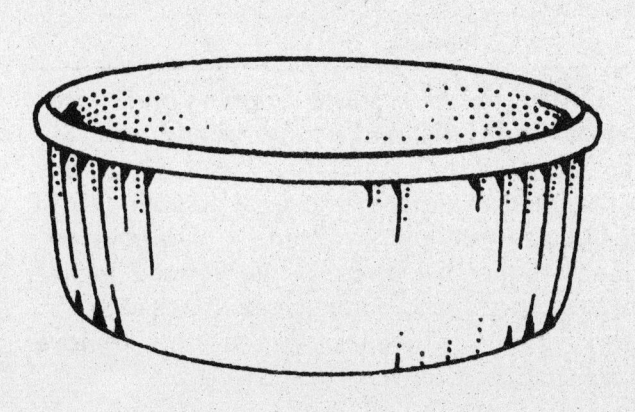

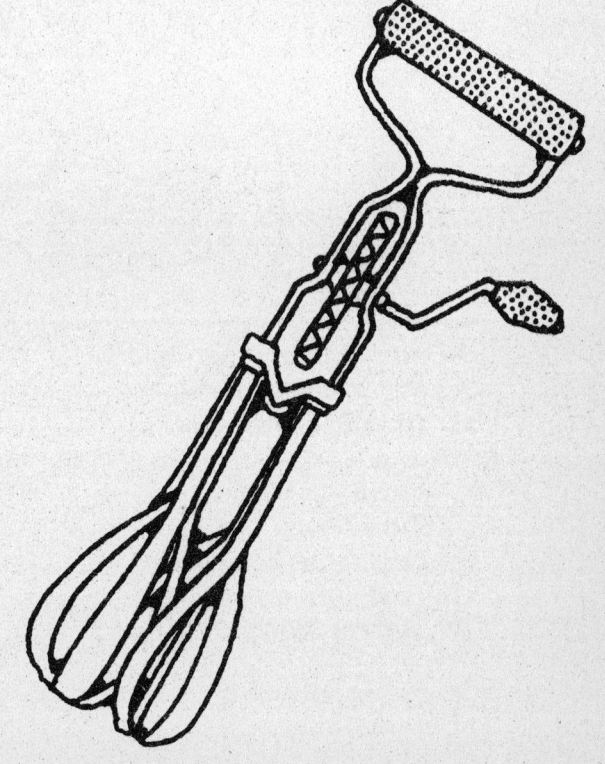

Cookies

Crisp Chocolate Rolls
Makes about 3 dozen

½ cup butter, softened
½ cup sugar
1 teaspoon vanilla
2 egg whites
⅔ cup all-purpose flour
  Creamy Chocolate Filling

In a large mixing bowl, cream butter, sugar, and vanilla until light and fluffy. Add egg whites; blend well. Gradually add flour; blend well. Drop batter by teaspoonfuls 1 inch apart on an ungreased baking sheet. Spread with the back of a spoon into 3-inch rounds. Bake at 375° F. for 5 minutes or until edges are light brown. Working with 1 cookie at a time, loosen from baking sheet with a spatula and then quickly roll tightly around a pencil. Transfer to a wire rack to cool, seam side down. With a pastry bag, soda straw, or wooden pick, fill rolls with Creamy Chocolate Filling.

Creamy Chocolate Filling

3 squares (1 ounce each) semisweet chocolate
¼ teaspoon vegetable oil, butter, *or* margarine

In a small saucepan, melt chocolate and oil over low heat, stirring constantly.

Cookies

Grandma's Peanut Butter Cookies
Makes about 5 dozen

- 1 cup butter *or* margarine
- 1 cup peanut butter
- 1 cup granulated sugar
- 1 cup packed brown sugar
- 2 eggs, lightly beaten
- 1 teaspoon vanilla
- 2 cups flour
- 1 teaspoon salt
- 1 teaspoon baking soda

In a mixing bowl, cream butter and peanut butter until well blended. Add sugars; cream until light and fluffy. Beat in eggs and vanilla. In a separate bowl, sift together flour, salt, and baking soda. Gradually add to creamed mixture; blend well. Roll dough into 1-inch balls. Place balls, 2 inches apart, on a large baking sheet. Press with tines of a fork to flatten. Bake at 350° F. about 10 minutes or until golden. Cool on a wire rack.

Chocolate Pecan Tarts
Makes about 4 dozen

- ½ cup butter *or* margarine, softened
- 2 packages (3 ounces each) cream cheese, softened
- ½ cup vegetable shortening
- 2 cups all-purpose flour
- Chocolate Pecan Filling

In a large mixing bowl, cream butter, cream cheese, and shortening until smooth. Gradually add flour; blend well. Cover and chill until firm. Shape dough into 1-inch balls. Place balls in ungreased miniature muffin cups. Press firmly onto bottom and up sides of muffin cups, set aside. Prepare Chocolate Pecan Filling. Spoon a heaping teaspoonful of filling into each tart shell. Bake at 350° F. for 20 to 25 minutes or until tarts are golden brown. Cool in pan on a wire rack.

Chocolate Pecan Filling

- 2 eggs
- ¾ cup sugar
- 3 tablespoons cornstarch
- ½ cup butter *or* margarine, melted
- 1 teaspoon vanilla
- 2 tablespoons light corn syrup
- ¾ cup miniature semisweet chocolate chips
- ½ cup finely chopped pecans

In a small bowl, combine eggs, sugar, and cornstarch; blend well. Blend in butter, vanilla, and corn syrup. Stir in chocolate chips and pecans.

Desserts

Fruit Bars
Makes 2 dozen

- ½ cup butter, softened
- 1 cup sugar
- 2 eggs
- 1 teaspoon vanilla
- ¾ cup all-purpose flour
- 1 teaspoon baking powder
- ¼ teaspoon salt
- 1 cup chopped walnuts
- ½ cup red candied cherries, halved
- 1 cup sliced pitted dates
- ½ cup sliced soft dried apricots
- ½ cup sliced soft dried figs
- Chocolate Glaze

In a large mixing bowl, cream butter and sugar until smooth. Add eggs, 1 at a time, beating well after each addition. Blend in vanilla. In another bowl, stir together flour, baking powder, and salt. Gradually add dry ingredients to creamed mixture; blend well. Stir in nuts and fruit. Spread batter in a greased 9-inch square baking pan. Bake at 350° F. for 45 minutes. Cool in pan before cutting into bars. Spread with Chocolate Glaze. Store in an airtight container.

Chocolate Glaze

- ⅓ cup sugar
- 3 tablespoons water
- 1 cup semisweet chocolate chips
- 3 tablespoons marshmallow creme
- 1 to 2 tablespoons hot water

In a small saucepan, combine sugar and 3 tablespoons water. Bring to a boil; remove from heat. Stir in chocolate chips until melted. Blend in marshmallow creme. Add hot water, 1 teaspoonful at a time, stirring until desired consistency is reached.

Desserts

CHERRY-OATMEAL COBBLER

Makes 6 servings

- 1 package (16 ounces) frozen unsweetened pitted tart red cherries, thawed
- ¾ cup sugar
- 1 tablespoon cornstarch
- 1 tablespoon butter or margarine
- ¼ teaspoon almond extract
- ⅓ roll refrigerated oatmeal cookie dough

Drain cherries, reserving juice; set cherries aside. If needed, add water to juice to make ½ cup. In a saucepan, combine sugar and cornstarch; stir in juice. Cook and stir over medium heat until thick and bubbly; stir in reserved cherries, butter and almond extract. Heat and stir until bubbly. Cut cookie dough into 6 slices. Turn hot cherry mixture into a 1½-quart casserole. Top with cookie dough slices. Bake at 400° for about 20 minutes or until bubbly.

Raspberry Bars

Makes 2 dozen

- ¾ cup margarine, softened
- 1 cup packed light brown sugar
- 1¾ cups all-purpose flour
- ½ teaspoon baking soda
- ½ teaspoon salt
- 1½ cups rolled oats
- 1 jar (18 ounces) raspberry jam

In a large mixing bowl, cream margarine and brown sugar until smooth. In another bowl, stir together flour, baking soda, and salt. Gradually add dry ingredients to creamed mixture; mix until crumbly. Stir in oats. Press half of the crumb mixture into a greased 13 x 9-inch baking pan. Spread with raspberry jam. Sprinkle remaining crumb mixture over the top; press lightly into jam. Bake at 400° F. for 20 minutes or until lightly browned. Cool 5 minutes before cutting into bars.

Desserts

STIRRED RICE PUDDING

Makes 4 servings

- 2 eggs, beaten
- 1 cup milk
- ¼ cup sugar
- ¼ cup raisins
- 1 cup cooked rice
- 1 teaspoon vanilla
- Dash salt
- Dash cinnamon

In a saucepan, combine eggs, milk, sugar and raisins. Cook and stir over medium heat for 6 to 8 minutes or until mixture coats a metal spoon. Remove from heat; stir in rice, vanilla, salt and cinnamon. Spoon into dessert dishes. Chill until serving time.

Light Nut Brownies

Makes 3 dozen

- ¼ butter *or* margarine, softened
- 1 cup all-purpose flour
- ¼ teaspoon salt
- 2 eggs
- ¾ cup packed light brown sugar
- 1 cup chopped walnuts, divided
- 1 teaspoon vanilla
- 2 tablespoons all-purpose flour
- Chocolate Frosting

In a large mixing bowl, cream butter. Gradually add 1 cup flour and salt; blend well. Spread the batter in a greased and floured 9-inch square baking pan. Bake at 350° F. for 15 minutes; cool. In a small bowl, beat eggs and sugar until light. Stir in ¾ cup nuts, vanilla, and 2 tablespoons flour. Spoon over cooled crust. Return to oven. Bake at 350° F. for 15 minutes. Cool in pan. Spread with Chocolate Frosting. Sprinkle with remaining ¼ cup nuts. Cut into squares.

Chocolate Frosting

- 1 cup semisweet chocolate chips
- ¼ cup light corn syrup
- 1 tablespoon water

In the top of a double boiler, melt chocolate chips over hot but not boiling water. Blend in corn syrup and water.

Desserts

Almond Squares
Makes 2½ dozen

- 3½ to 4 cups flour
- 1 package active dry yeast
- ⅔ cup sugar, divided
- ¼ teaspoon salt
- 1 cup milk, lukewarm
- ¾ cup butter *or* margarine, melted, cooled to lukewarm, and divided
- 2 teaspoons vanilla, divided
- ½ cup flaked almonds
- Sugar

Sift flour into a large bowl; sprinkle yeast over flour and mix well. Blend in ⅓ cup sugar, salt, milk, ¼ cup butter, and 1 teaspoon vanilla. Add more flour if the dough becomes sticky, but dough should remain soft. Place dough on a lightly floured board and knead until smooth. Move dough to a greased bowl; turn once to grease lightly. Cover bowl and put in a warm place for 1½ hours or until dough doubles in bulk. Punch down, and turn out onto a lightly floured board; knead until smooth. Roll out dough to fit a greased 10 x 15-inch cookie sheet; place on cookie sheet. Brush remaining butter over dough. Combine remaining sugar and vanilla; sprinkle over dough. Sprinkle on almonds. Cover and let rise for 45 minutes or until doubled in bulk. Bake in a preheated 350° F. oven for 35 minutes or until golden brown. Sprinkle with sugar. Remove from sheet and cool on wire rack. Cut into squares.

FRESH PEACH COMPOTE
Makes 4 servings

- 2 tablespoons light corn syrup
- 2 tablespoons frozen lemonade concentrate, thawed
- 2 tablespoons orange liqueur
- 3 medium peaches

Combine corn syrup, lemonade concentrate and liqueur; set aside. Peel, pit and slice peaches. Pour syrup mixture over peaches; stir thoroughly to coat. Cover and chill. Stir again before serving.

Desserts

Irish Mist Bars
Makes 1½ dozen

½ cup butter, softened
1½ cups packed light brown sugar, divided
1 cup all-purpose flour
1 tablespoon all-purpose flour
¼ teaspoon salt
2 eggs
1 tablespoon Irish Mist liqueur
1 cup chopped nuts

In a large mixing bowl, combine butter, ½ cup brown sugar, and 1 cup flour; blend until crumbly. Firmly press crumb mixture into a 9-inch square baking pan. Bake at 350° F. for 10 minutes; set aside to cool. In a large mixing bowl, combine remaining 1 cup brown sugar, 1 tablespoon flour, and salt; blend well. Add eggs, 1 at a time, beating well after each addition. Blend in liqueur; stir in nuts. Spread batter evenly over cooled crust. Bake at 350° F. for 20 minutes. Cool in pan before cutting into bars.

MELON MELBA
Makes 4 servings

1 package (10 ounces) frozen raspberries (in quick-thaw pouch), thawed
1 to 2 tablespoons sugar
1 teaspoon cornstarch
3 cups cubed honeydew melon

Drain raspberries; reserve juice. In a small saucepan, combine sugar and cornstarch; stir in reserved juice. Cook and stir over medium heat until thick and bubbly; cook and stir for 2 minutes more. Remove from heat; stir in berries. Cool. To serve, spoon melon into dessert dishes; top with berry sauce.

Desserts

Filbert Chocolate Cream Bars
Makes 3 dozen

- 1 cup chopped filberts *or* almonds
- ½ cup butter
- ¼ cup sugar
- 2 tablespoons unsweetened cocoa
- 2 teaspoons vanilla
- ¼ teaspoon salt
- 1 egg, beaten
- 1¾ cups vanilla wafer crumbs (about 45 wafers)
- ½ cup flaked coconut
- Mint Frosting
- 4 squares (1 ounce each) semisweet baking chocolate

Spread nuts in a shallow baking pan. Toast in oven for 5 to 10 minutes, stirring occasionally. In a medium saucepan, combine butter, sugar, cocoa, vanilla, salt, and egg. Cook over low heat, stirring constantly until mixture thickens and becomes glossy. Combine cookie crumbs, nuts, and coconut. Add cocoa mixture; blend well. Press firmly into a 9-inch square baking pan. Spread Mint Frosting on top. Chill until frosting is firm. In the top of a double boiler, melt chocolate over hot but not boiling water. Spread chocolate over frosting. Let stand until chocolate is partially set. Cut into bars. Refrigerate until ready to serve.

Mint Frosting

- ¼ cup butter, softened
- 1 egg
- ½ teaspoon peppermint extract
- 2 cups sifted powdered sugar

In a small mixing bowl, cream butter and egg until smooth. Blend in peppermint extract. Gradually add powdered sugar, beating until smooth and creamy.

STRAWBERRIES WITH CREAM
Makes 4 servings

- 2 cups fresh strawberries, quartered
- 2 tablespoons sugar
- ½ of a 4-ounce container frozen whipped dessert topping, thawed
- ¼ cup sour cream
- ⅛ teaspoon cinnamon

Sprinkle strawberries with 1 tablespoon of sugar; cover and chill. In a bowl, combine dessert topping, sour cream, cinnamon and remaining sugar. To serve, spoon strawberries into dessert dishes; top with cream mixture.

Desserts

Rhubarb Custard Dessert
Makes one 18 x 12-inch pie

Crust (recipe follows)
6 eggs, separated
2¾ cups sugar, divided
1 cup half-and-half *or* milk*
¼ cup flour
6 cups chopped rhubarb
½ cup chopped nuts, optional
½ cup shredded coconut, optional

Prepare crust; pat into an 18 x 12-inch baking pan. Bake at 350° F. 10 minutes. Remove from oven; let stand until cool. In a large mixing bowl, combine egg yolks, 2 cups sugar, half-and-half, and flour; blend well. Stir in rhubarb. Pour custard mixture evenly over cooled crust. Bake at 350° F. 40 minutes or until set. In a small mixing bowl, beat egg whites with an electric mixer until foamy. Gradually add remaining ¾ cup sugar, beating until stiff peaks form. Spread meringue on top of rhubarb custard, being certain to seal edges. Sprinkle with nuts and coconut, if desired. Bake 10 to 12 minutes or until lightly browned.

*If using milk, add 1 whole egg to custard.

Crust

1 cup vegetable shortening
2 cups flour
2 tablespoons sugar

In a mixing bowl, cut shortening into flour and sugar using a pastry blender or two knives until consistency of coarse crumbs.

Spice Bars
Makes about 2 dozen

1 cup water
1 cup sugar
1 cup raisins
½ cup butter
Salt, to taste
2 cups flour
1 teaspoon baking soda
1 teaspoon cinnamon
½ teaspoon nutmeg
½ teaspoon cloves
½ cup chopped dates
½ cup walnuts, chopped
Powdered sugar

In a saucepan, mix first 5 ingredients and bring to a boil; let cool. In a bowl, mix flour, baking soda, and spices. Combine the cooled raisin mixture with the flour mixture. Add the dates and walnuts. Spread on a greased 13 x 9-inch cookie sheet and bake in a preheated 350° F. oven 25 minutes. Sprinkle with powdered sugar while warm.

Desserts

Double Chocolate Crumble Bars
Makes about 4 dozen

- ½ cup butter, softened
- ¾ cup sugar
- 2 eggs
- 1 teaspoon vanilla
- ¾ cup all-purpose flour
- ½ cup chopped pecans
- 2 tablespoons unsweetened cocoa
- ¼ teaspoon baking powder
- ¼ teaspoon salt
- 2 cups miniature marshmallows
- 1 package (6 ounces) semisweet chocolate chips
- 1 cup peanut butter
- 1½ cups crispy rice cereal

In a large mixing bowl, cream butter and sugar until smooth. Blend in eggs and vanilla. Stir together flour, pecans, cocoa, baking powder, and salt. Gradually add dry ingredients to the creamed mixture; blend well. Spread batter in a greased 13 x 9-inch baking pan. Bake at 350° F. for 15 to 20 minutes or until light brown. Sprinkle marshmallows evenly over top. Bake for 3 minutes. Cool in pan on a wire rack. In a small saucepan, melt chocolate chips and peanut butter over low heat, stirring constantly. Stir in cereal. Spread on top of cooled crust. Refrigerate until firm. Cut into bars. Store in the refrigerator.

FRESH FRUIT WITH MARMALADE CREAM
Makes 4 servings

- ⅓ cup sour cream
- 1 tablespoon orange marmalade
- Dash nutmeg
- 3 cups mixed fresh fruit (sliced strawberries, sliced bananas, blueberries, or pineapple chunks)

Combine sour cream, marmalade and nutmeg. Spoon fruit into dessert dishes; top with sour cream mixture.

Desserts

Moist Chocolate Brownies
Makes 1½ dozen

- 1 box (8 ounces) semisweet chocolate
- 7 tablespoons butter
- 2 eggs
- ¾ cup sugar
- 1 teaspoon vanilla
- ¼ cup all-purpose flour
- 1 cup coarsely chopped walnuts

In the top of a double boiler, melt chocolate and butter over warm water. Remove from heat. In a large mixing bowl, beat eggs and sugar until light and fluffy. Blend in chocolate mixture and vanilla. Stir in flour and nuts. Pour batter into a greased 8-inch square baking pan. Bake at 375° F. for 30 minutes or until brownie begins to pull away from sides of the pan. Cool in pan before cutting into squares.

PEACH COBBLER
Makes 4 servings

- ½ cup biscuit mix
- 1 tablespoon sugar
- 1 tablespoon milk
- 1 teaspoon cooking oil
- 1 teaspoon butter or margarine, softened
- 1 tablespoon sugar
- ½ teaspoon cinnamon
- 1 can (16 ounces) sliced peaches
- 3 tablespoons sugar
- 2 teaspoons cornstarch
- 2 teaspoons lemon juice

Stir together biscuit mix and 1 tablespoon sugar. Add milk and cooking oil; mix well. On a floured surface, pat biscuit dough to a 6 x 4-inch rectangle. Spread with butter, then sprinkle with 1 tablespoon sugar and cinnamon. Roll up jelly-roll style, starting at the narrow side. Cut into fourths.

Drain peaches, reserving syrup. Add water to syrup to make 1 cup. In a saucepan, combine 3 tablespoons sugar and cornstarch. Stir in syrup mixture. Cook and stir over medium heat until thick and bubbly. Stir in peaches and lemon juice; return to boiling.

Divide peach mixture among four 1-cup baking dishes. Top each with a biscuit. Bake at 425° about 15 minutes or until biscuits are golden.

Desserts

Orange Bars
Makes 3 dozen

½ cup butter, softened
1½ cups all-purpose flour
¼ cup sugar
3 tablespoons grated orange peel
1 egg
1 package (6 ounces) semisweet chocolate chips

In a large mixing bowl, cut butter into flour until crumbly. Blend in sugar, orange peel, and egg. Roll out dough on a lightly floured surface to a ¼-inch thickness. Cut into 2 x 1-inch bars. Place bars about 1 inch apart on a lightly greased baking sheet. Bake at 400° F. for 8 to 10 minutes or until lightly browned. Remove from baking sheet to a wire rack to cool. Melt chocolate in the top of a double boiler over hot but not boiling water. Dip each bar halfway into the melted chocolate. Place on a sheet of waxed paper until the chocolate sets, about 10 minutes.

Chocolate Chip Butterscotch Bars
Makes 2 dozen

¾ cup all-purpose flour
½ teaspoon baking powder
½ teaspoon salt
½ cup butter *or* margarine
1 cup packed dark brown sugar
2 eggs
1 teaspoon vanilla
2½ cups semisweet chocolate chips, divided
½ cup chopped walnuts
Butterscotch Frosting

Stir together flour, baking powder, and salt; set aside. In a medium saucepan, melt butter. Add brown sugar; stir over low heat until sugar melts. Transfer to a large mixing bowl. Add eggs, 1 at a time, beating well after each addition. Blend in vanilla. Add dry ingredients; blend well. Stir in 2 cups chocolate chips and nuts. Spread batter in a greased 8-inch square baking pan. Bake at 350° F. for 30 minutes. Cool in pan. Frost with Butterscotch Frosting. Sprinkle with remaining ½ cup chocolate chips. Cut into bars.

Butterscotch Frosting

¼ cup butter *or* margarine, softened
½ cup packed dark brown sugar
1 tablespoon half-and-half
¼ teaspoon vanilla

In a small mixing bowl, cream butter and sugar until smooth. Blend in cream and vanilla. If frosting is too soft to spread, chill 10 minutes before using.

Desserts

Pear and Graham Cracker Bars
Makes about 2½ dozen

- 2 ripe Bartlett pears
- Whole graham crackers
- 1 cup packed light brown sugar
- ½ cup butter *or* margarine
- ¼ cup milk
- 1 cup flaked coconut
- 1 cup graham cracker crumbs
- 1 package (6 ounces) butterscotch chips

Core and dice pears to measure 1½ cups. Line a 13 x 9-inch baking pan with whole graham crackers. In a medium saucepan, combine diced pears, brown sugar, butter, milk, coconut, and graham cracker crumbs; bring to a boil. Boil until thick, stirring constantly. Spread pear mixture over crackers. Top with layer of whole crackers. In the top of a double boiler, melt butterscotch chips. Spread melted chips over crackers. Cut between crackers into bars. Store in the refrigerator.

APPLE-BLUEBERRY CRISP
Makes 6 servings

- 1 can (21 ounces) apple pie filling
- 1 cup fresh *or* frozen blueberries
- 1 teaspoon lemon juice
- ¼ cup quick-cooking rolled oats
- ¼ cup flour
- ¼ cup brown sugar
- ½ teaspoon cinnamon
- ¼ cup butter *or* margarine
- Vanilla ice cream, optional

Combine pie filling, blueberries and lemon juice; turn into a 9-inch pie plate. In a bowl, combine oats, flour, brown sugar and cinnamon; cut in butter until mixture resembles coarse crumbs. Sprinkle over fruit. Bake at 350° for 25 to 30 minutes or until bubbly. Serve warm with vanilla ice cream, if desired.

Desserts

Peanut Brittle Bars
Makes 3 dozen

- 1 cup all-purpose flour
- ¼ teaspoon baking soda
- ½ teaspoon cinnamon
- ½ cup butter, softened
- ½ cup packed light brown sugar
- 1 teaspoon vanilla
- 1 egg, beaten
- 1 cup finely chopped salted peanuts, divided

Sift together flour, baking soda, and cinnamon; set aside. In a large mixing bowl, cream butter and brown sugar until smooth. Blend in vanilla and 2 tablespoons of the egg; reserve remaining egg. Gradually add dry ingredients, blending well. Stir in ½ cup peanuts. Spread batter in a greased 14 x 10-inch baking pan. Brush with reserved egg. Sprinkle with remaining ½ cup peanuts. Bake at 325° F. for 20 minutes. Cool in pan 5 minutes before cutting into bars.

PEACH SUNDAE CRUNCH

Makes 4 servings

- ¼ cup quick-cooking rolled oats
- ¼ cup brown sugar
- 2 tablespoons butter or margarine, melted
- ¼ teaspoon cinnamon
- 1 can (16 ounces) peach slices, chilled
- Vanilla ice cream

In a shallow baking pan, combine oats, brown sugar, butter and cinnamon; spread mixture evenly over the bottom of the pan. Bake at 350° for 10 minutes. Remove from the oven; stir occasionally to break into small pieces as crumb mixture cools. To serve, spoon peaches into dessert dishes; top with a scoop of ice cream. Sprinkle with crumb mixture.

Desserts

Pumpkin Bars
Makes 3 dozen

- 4 eggs
- 1 cup vegetable oil
- 2 cups sugar
- 1 can (15 ounces) pumpkin
- 2 cups flour
- 2 teaspoons baking powder
- 1 teaspoon baking soda
- ½ teaspoon salt
- 2 teaspoons ground cinnamon
- ½ teaspoon ground ginger
- ½ teaspoon ground cloves
- ½ teaspoon ground nutmeg
- ½ cup chopped nuts
- Cream Cheese Frosting

In a large bowl, combine eggs, oil, sugar, and pumpkin; blend well. In a separate bowl, sift together flour, baking powder, baking soda, salt, and spices. Gradually beat flour mixture into pumpkin mixture. Stir in nuts. Pour batter into greased and floured 18 x 12-inch pan. Bake at 350° F. 25 to 30 minutes or until center springs back when touched lightly. Cool on a wire rack before frosting with Creamed Cheese Frosting.

Cream Cheese Frosting

- 6 ounces cream cheese, softened
- 6 tablespoons butter *or* margarine, softened
- 1 tablespoon milk
- 1 teaspoon vanilla
- 4 cups sifted powdered sugar

In a mixing bowl, combine cream cheese and butter; cream until light and fluffy. Beat in milk and vanilla. Gradually beat in powdered sugar until of spreading consistency.

GERMAN OVEN PANCAKE
Makes 4 servings

- 6 eggs
- 1 cup milk
- ¼ cup butter *or* margarine, melted
- 1 cup flour
- ¾ teaspoon salt
- Melted butter *or* margarine
- Sifted powdered sugar

In a blender, combine eggs, milk and melted butter. Cover and blend on low speed until mixed. Add flour and salt; cover and blend on medium speed until smooth. Pour into well-greased 13 x 9 x 2-inch baking dish. Bake at 450° for 20 to 22 minutes or until puffed and golden brown. Drizzle with melted butter and sprinkle with powdered sugar. Serve immediately.

Desserts

BANANAS WITH RUM CREAM

Makes 4 servings

1 egg, separated
¼ cup brown sugar
1 tablespoon dark rum
½ of a 4-ounce container frozen whipped dessert topping, thawed
4 small bananas, sliced
Chocolate curls, optional

In a small mixer bowl, beat egg white until soft peaks form; gradually add half of the brown sugar, beating until stiff peaks form. Transfer to a clean bowl. In the same mixer bowl, beat egg yolk until thick and lemon colored; beat in remaining brown sugar and rum. Fold egg white and dessert topping into yolk mixture. Chill until serving time. To serve, place sliced bananas in 4 dessert dishes. Spoon rum cream over fruit. Garnish with chocolate curls, if desired.

Best Fudge Nut Brownies
Makes 1 dozen

4 squares (1 ounce each) unsweetened baking chocolate
1 cup butter *or* margarine
2 cups sugar
3 eggs, lightly beaten
2 teaspoons vanilla
½ teaspoon salt
1 cup chopped nuts
1 cup sifted flour

Preheat oven to 350° F. In a small saucepan, melt chocolate and butter over low heat, stirring constantly. Add sugar and eggs; blend well. Stir in vanilla, salt, and nuts. Gradually add flour; blend well. Pour into a greased and floured 9-inch square baking pan. Bake 40 to 45 minutes or until brownie begins to pull away from edge of pan. Cool in pan on a wire rack. Cut into squares.

Desserts

Blonde Brownies
Makes 1½ dozen

- ½ cup butter, softened
- 1 cup sugar
- 1 egg yolk
- 1 whole egg
- 1 teaspoon vanilla
- 2 cups all-purpose flour
- 1 teaspoon baking powder
- ½ teaspoon salt
- 1 cup packed brown sugar
- 1 cup chopped walnuts
- 1 egg white

In a large mixing bowl, cream butter and sugar until smooth. Add egg yolk, whole egg, and vanilla; blend well. Sift together flour, baking powder, and salt. Gradually add to creamed mixture, beating until well blended. Pour batter into a greased 9-inch square baking pan. Stir together brown sugar, nuts, and egg white. Spread over the batter. Bake at 325° F. for 1 hour or until brownie begins to pull away from sides of the pan. Cool in pan before cutting into squares.

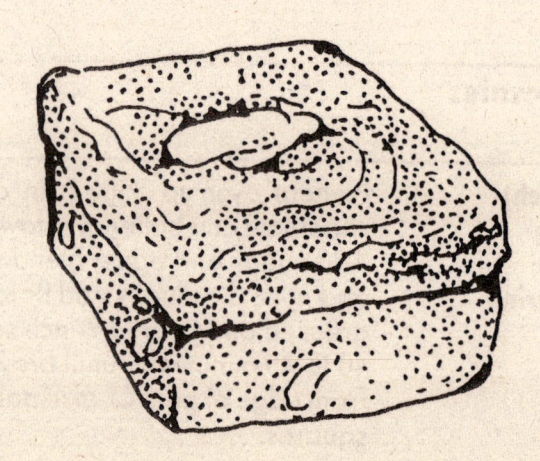

ALMOND-FUDGE BARS
Makes 20 bars

- ½ cup butter or margarine
- 2 squares unsweetened chocolate
- 1 cup sugar
- 2 eggs
- ½ teaspoon almond extract
- ¾ cup flour
- ½ cup semi-sweet chocolate pieces
- ⅓ cup chopped almonds

In a saucepan, melt butter and unsweetened chocolate over low heat. Remove from heat and stir in sugar. Add eggs, one at a time, beating well. Stir in almond extract. Add flour; mix well. Stir in chocolate pieces and almonds. Spread in a greased 8 x 8 x 2-inch baking pan. Bake at 350° for 30 minutes. Cool; cut into squares.

Desserts

CHOCOLATE CAKE WITH BROILED ICING

Makes 4 or 5 servings

- 1 frozen unfrosted chocolate cake (1 layer)
- ¼ cup brown sugar
- ¼ cup chopped nuts
- 3 tablespoons butter *or* margarine, softened
- 2 tablespoons whipping cream

Place frozen cake on a baking sheet. Combine brown sugar, nuts, butter and whipping cream; spread over frozen cake. Let stand for 30 minutes. Just before serving, preheat broiler. Broil cake 4 inches from heat about 1 minute or until frosting is bubbly. Serve immediately.

Two-Toned Brownies

Makes about 1½ dozen

- ¼ cup butter *or* margarine, softened
- ¼ cup sugar
- ¼ cup light corn syrup
- 1 egg
- 1 cup all-purpose flour
- ½ teaspoon baking powder
- ¼ teaspoon salt
- 2 squares (1 ounce each) semisweet chocolate, melted
- 1 package (3 ounces) cream cheese, softened

In a large mixing bowl, cream butter and sugar until smooth. Blend in corn syrup and egg. Combine flour, baking powder, and salt. Add dry ingredients to creamed mixture; blend well. To ½ cup of the batter blend in melted chocolate. To remaining batter, add cream cheese; beat until smooth. Spread cream cheese batter in a greased 9-inch square baking pan. Carefully spread chocolate batter on top. With a knife, swirl chocolate batter through cream cheese batter. Bake at 350° F. for 40 to 45 minutes or until brownie begins to pull away from sides of the pan. Cool in pan before cutting into squares.

Desserts

SAUTÉED APPLES
Makes 4 servings

4 medium apples, sliced
2 tablespoons butter or margarine
2 tablespoons sugar
 Dash cinnamon

In a skillet, cook and stir apples in hot butter over medium-high heat for 6 to 8 minutes or until tender. Stir in sugar and cinnamon. Serve hot.

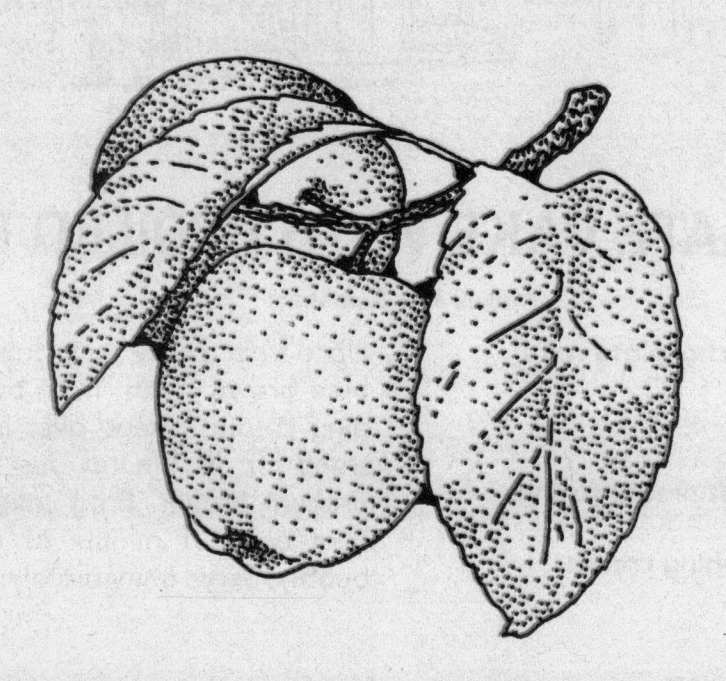

Toffee Crunch Brownies
Makes 2 dozen

---

4 squares (1 ounce each) unsweetened baking chocolate
½ cup butter
4 eggs
1 cup sugar
2 teaspoons vanilla
¾ cup all-purpose flour
¼ teaspoon salt
6 ounces toffee candy bars, chopped

In the top of a double boiler, melt chocolate and butter over warm water. Remove from heat. In a large mixing bowl, beat eggs and sugar until light and fluffy; blend into chocolate mixture. Blend in vanilla, flour, and salt. Stir in toffee candy. Spoon mixture into a greased 9-inch square baking pan. Bake at 325° F. for 45 minutes. Cool in pan before cutting into squares.

Desserts

CHOCOLATE-MARSHMALLOW PUDDING

Makes 4 servings

10 marshmallows
¼ cup milk
1 bar (3¾ ounces) milk chocolate
1 container (4 ounces) frozen whipped dessert topping, thawed

In the top of a double boiler, heat marshmallows and milk over hot water until melted; add chocolate and stir until melted and smooth. Transfer to a metal bowl; chill in the refrigerator, about 15 minutes or until cooled, stirring occasionally. Fold in whipped topping. Spoon into dessert dishes. Place in the freezer until serving time.

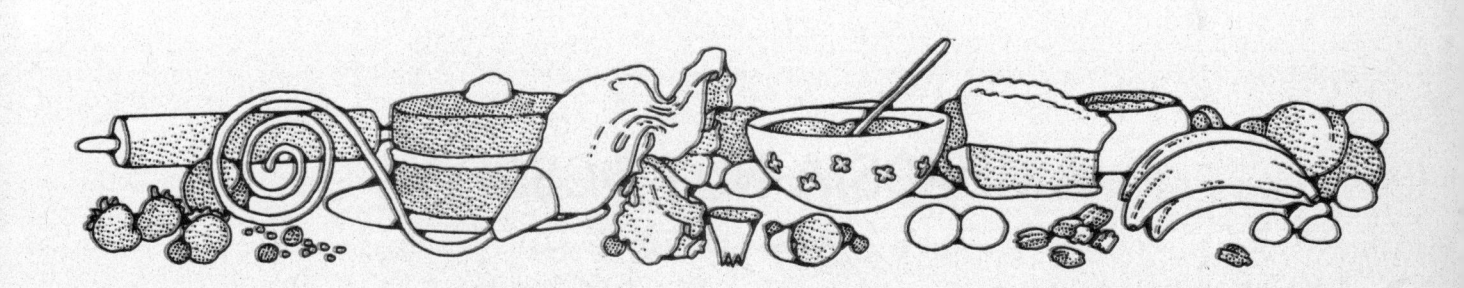

English Toffee Bars

Makes about 6 dozen

1 cup butter, softened
1 cup sugar
1 egg yolk
1¾ cups all-purpose flour
1 teaspoon cinnamon
1 egg white, lightly beaten
1 cup chopped pecans
3 tablespoons milk
1 teaspoon instant coffee granules
2 squares (1 ounce each) semisweet chocolate

In a large bowl, cream butter and sugar until smooth. Add egg yolk; blend well. Sift together flour and cinnamon. Gradually work dry ingredients into creamed mixture until crumbly. Press crumb mixture evenly into a buttered 15 x 10-inch baking pan. Brush top with egg white. Sprinkle with pecans; press lightly into dough. Bake at 275° F. for 1 hour. While the crust is baking, heat milk, coffee granules, and chocolate in a saucepan over low heat, stirring until chocolate melts. Cut into 1½-inch bars. Drizzle with melted chocolate mixture. Cool in pan on a wire rack.

Desserts

Date Chocolate Chip Bars
Makes 1 dozen

- 1 package (8 ounces) pitted dates, chopped
- ½ cup sugar
- 1 cup water
- ⅔ cup butter *or* margarine
- 1 cup packed brown sugar
- 1½ cups quick-cooking oats
- 1 teaspoon baking soda
- 1 tablespoon hot water
- 1½ cups flour
- ½ cup chopped nuts
- ½ cup semisweet chocolate chips
- Sweetened whipped cream, optional

In a medium saucepan, combine dates, sugar, and water. Cook over medium heat until thick, stirring constantly. In a mixing bowl, combine butter and brown sugar. Cream with an electric mixer until light and fluffy. Add oats, baking soda, and hot water; blend well. Gradually add flour; blend well. Reserve 1 cup oat mixture for topping. Press remaining mixture into an ungreased 13 x 9-inch baking pan. Spread date mixture evenly over top. Sprinkle with nuts, chocolate chips, and reserved mixture; pat lightly. Bake at 350° F. 20 to 25 minutes or until golden. Serve warm or cool topped with whipped cream, if desired.

AMBROSIA-NUT DESSERT
Makes 4 servings

- 2 tablespoons shredded coconut
- 1 tablespoon finely chopped pecans
- 1 tablespoon butter *or* margarine, melted
- 1 cup fresh pineapple chunks
- 1 cup seedless green grapes, halved
- ½ cup fresh blueberries

In a shallow baking pan, combine coconut, pecans and butter. Bake at 350° for 5 to 6 minutes or until lightly toasted, stirring occasionally. Cool. Combine pineapple, grapes and blueberries; add coconut mixture. Toss lightly. Spoon into dessert dishes.

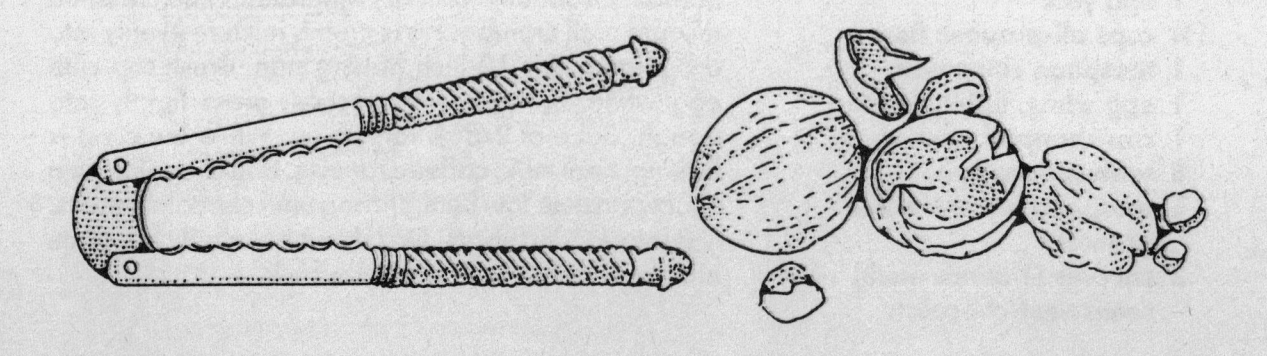

Desserts

Marshmallow Pecan Brownies
Makes 3 dozen

- 2 squares (1 ounce each) unsweetened baking chocolate
- ½ cup butter *or* margarine
- 2 eggs
- 1 cup sugar
- 1 teaspoon vanilla
- 1¼ cups sifted all-purpose flour
- ½ teaspoon baking powder
- ½ teaspoon salt
- 1 cup chopped pecans
- 2 cups miniature marshmallows
- Mocha Chocolate Frosting

In a small saucepan, melt chocolate and butter over low heat, stirring constantly; set aside to cool. In a large mixing bowl, beat eggs lightly. Blend in sugar, vanilla, and melted chocolate mixture. Stir together flour, baking powder, and salt; gradually blend into chocolate mixture. Stir in pecans. Spread batter in a greased 11 x 7-inch baking pan. Bake at 325° F. for 25 minutes or until brownie begins to pull away from sides of the pan. Sprinkle marshmallows evenly over top. Return to oven for 3 to 4 minutes or until marshmallows are soft. Cool before spreading with Mocha Chocolate Frosting. Cut into 2 x 1-inch bars.

Mocha Chocolate Frosting

- 1 square (1 ounce) unsweetened chocolate
- 2 tablespoons butter
- 1 teaspoon instant coffee granules
- ½ teaspoon vanilla
- ⅛ teaspoon salt
- 2 cups powdered sugar
- 2 to 3 tablespoons hot water

In a small saucepan, melt chocolate and butter over low heat, stirring constantly. Blend in coffee, vanilla, and salt. Gradually beat in powdered sugar, adding water, if necessary, to bring to spreading consistency.

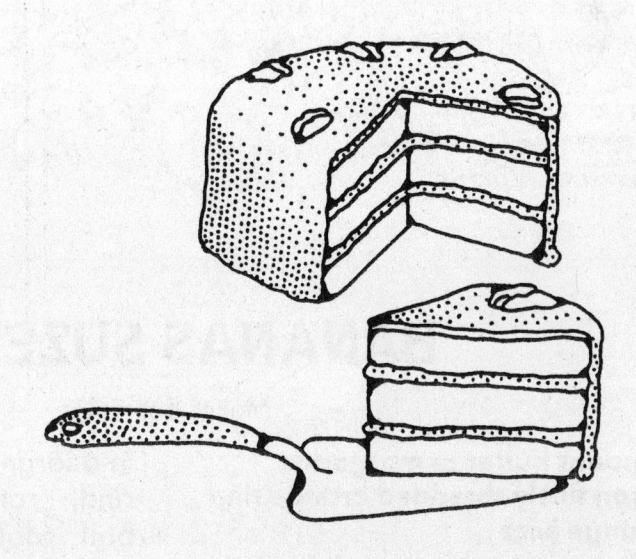

Desserts

Jeweled Coconut Chews
Makes about 1½ dozen

- ⅓ cup butter *or* margarine, softened
- ⅓ cup powdered sugar
- ¾ cup all-purpose flour
- 1 cup seedless green grapes
- ½ cup packed brown sugar
- ¼ cup chopped walnuts
- ¼ cup flaked coconut
- 1 tablespoon flour
- 1 egg
- ¼ teaspoon baking powder
- ¼ teaspoon salt
- ¼ teaspoon almond extract
- ⅛ teaspoon nutmeg

In a small mixing bowl, cream butter and powdered sugar until smooth. Add ¾ cup flour; mix until crumbly. Press crumb mixture into an ungreased 8-inch square baking pan. Bake at 350° F. for 15 minutes or until light brown. In a large bowl, combine remaining ingredients; blend well. Spread over baked crust. Bake at 350° F. for 25 minutes or until golden brown. Cool in pan before cutting into bars.

BANANAS SUZETTE
Makes 4 servings

- 3 tablespoons butter *or* margarine
- 1 teaspoon finely shredded orange rind
- ½ cup orange juice
- 6 tablespoons sugar
- 2 tablespoons orange liqueur
- 4 firm ripe bananas, halved lengthwise

In a large skillet, melt butter; stir in orange rind, orange juice and sugar. Bring to a boil; cook and stir for 4 to 5 minutes or until slightly thickened. Stir in liqueur. Add bananas; heat through, spooning sauce over bananas. Serve immediately.

Meat

SKILLET BARBECUES

Makes 8 sandwiches

1 pound ground beef
1 medium onion, chopped
½ cup catsup
½ cup chili sauce
1 tablespoon vinegar
1 teaspoon prepared mustard
1 teaspoon Worcestershire sauce
½ teaspoon sugar
¼ teaspoon celery salt
8 hamburger buns, split

In a skillet, cook ground beef and onion until meat is brown and onion is tender; drain thoroughly. Stir in catsup, chili sauce, vinegar, mustard, Worcestershire, sugar and celery salt. Simmer, uncovered, for 15 minutes. Spoon into hamburger buns.

BEEF STROGANOFF

Makes 6 servings

1 pound beef tenderloin or sirloin steak
2 tablespoons butter or margarine
2 cups sliced fresh mushrooms
½ cup chopped onion
½ cup water
2 teaspoons Worcestershire sauce
1 teaspoon instant beef bouillon granules
½ teaspoon salt
1 cup sour cream
2 tablespoons flour
Hot cooked noodles
Paprika

Slice beef thinly across the grain into bite-sized strips. In a medium skillet, brown meat in hot butter over medium-high heat, stirring occasionally. Add mushrooms and onion; sauté for 3 to 4 minutes or until onion is tender-crisp. Stir in water, Worcestershire, bouillon granules and salt; bring to a boil. In a small bowl, stir together sour cream and flour; stir into meat mixture. Cook and stir over medium heat until thick and bubbly; cook and stir for 1 minute more. Serve over hot noodles; sprinkle with paprika.

Beef

BEEF WITH PEPPERS AND TOMATOES

Makes 4 servings

1 pound beef tenderloin *or* sirloin steak
1 teaspoon cornstarch
½ teaspoon sugar
¼ teaspoon salt
2 tablespoons dry sherry
2 tablespoons soy sauce
2 tablespoons cooking oil
1 large green pepper, cut into strips
1 cup halved cherry tomatoes
Hot cooked rice

Slice beef thinly across the grain into bite-sized strips. In a small bowl, combine cornstarch, sugar and salt. Stir in sherry and soy sauce; set aside. Preheat a wok or large skillet over high heat; add oil. Stir-fry beef and green pepper in hot oil for 3 to 4 minutes or until meat is brown and pepper is tender-crisp. Stir cornstarch mixture; blend into meat mixture. Cook and stir until thick and bubbly. Stir in tomatoes. Cook and stir until heated through. Serve with rice.

STEAK AND ONIONS

Makes 4 servings

½ cup dry red *or* white wine
¼ cup soy sauce
Dash garlic powder
4 beef cube steaks, about 1 pound each
1 large onion, sliced and separated into rings
2 tablespoons butter *or* margarine
1 tablespoon cooking oil

In a large shallow baking dish, combine wine, soy sauce and garlic powder. Arrange steaks in a single layer in the baking dish; cover and marinate at room temperature, about 45 minutes. (Or, marinate in the refrigerator for 4 to 6 hours.) In a large skillet, cook and stir onion in hot butter over medium-high heat for 4 to 5 minutes or until tender. Remove from skillet; keep warm. Drain steaks. In the same skillet, cook steaks in hot oil over medium-high heat for 3 minutes; turn and cook for 2 to 3 minutes more or until done. Serve with onions.

Chicken

CHICKEN LIVERS IN PATTY SHELLS

Makes 4 servings

- 4 frozen patty shells
- 2 slices bacon
- 12 ounces chicken livers, coarsely chopped
- 1½ cups sliced fresh mushrooms
- ⅓ cup milk
- 1 teaspoon flour
- 1 package (3 ounces) cream cheese, cubed
- 1 teaspoon snipped chives
- 1 teaspoon Worcestershire sauce
- ½ teaspoon salt

Bake patty shells. In a skillet, fry bacon until crisp. Remove bacon and drain, reserving drippings in the skillet. Crumble bacon and set aside. In reserved drippings, cook chicken livers and mushrooms over medium-high heat for 6 to 8 minutes or until tender. Remove from skillet, reserving pan juices; keep warm. Blend milk and flour. In the same skillet, combine reserved pan juices, milk mixture, cream cheese, chives, Worcestershire and salt. Cook and stir until thick and bubbly. Add livers and mushrooms; cook and stir until heated through. Spoon into patty shells; sprinkle with reserved bacon.

CHICKEN STIR-FRY

Makes 4 servings

- 2 whole chicken breasts, skinned and boned
- 3 tablespoons cornstarch
- 1 tablespoon dry white wine
- 1 teaspoon sugar
- ½ teaspoon salt
- ½ cup chicken broth
- 3 tablespoons cooking oil
- 2 slices gingerroot
- 1½ cups sliced fresh mushrooms
- 2 stalks celery, diagonally sliced
- 6 green onions, sliced into 1-inch lengths
- 1½ cups bean sprouts
- Hot cooked rice

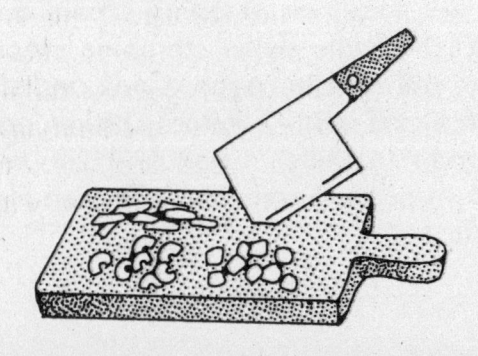

Cut chicken into 1-inch pieces. Sprinkle with 2 tablespoons of cornstarch and wine; mix well. Let stand at room temperature for 20 to 30 minutes. In a small bowl, combine remaining 1 tablespoon cornstarch, sugar and salt; stir in chicken broth. Set aside. Preheat wok or large skillet over high heat; add 2 tablespoons of oil and gingerroot. Heat until gingerroot begins to brown. Remove gingerroot and discard. Add chicken to wok; stir-fry in hot oil for 4 to 5 minutes or until tender. Remove from wok; keep warm. Heat remaining 1 tablespoon oil in wok; add mushrooms, celery and green onions. Stir-fry for 3 to 4 minutes or until tender-crisp. Return chicken to wok; stir in bean sprouts. Stir cornstarch mixture; blend into wok. Cook and stir until thick and bubbly. Cook and stir 1 to 2 minutes more. Serve with rice.

Chicken

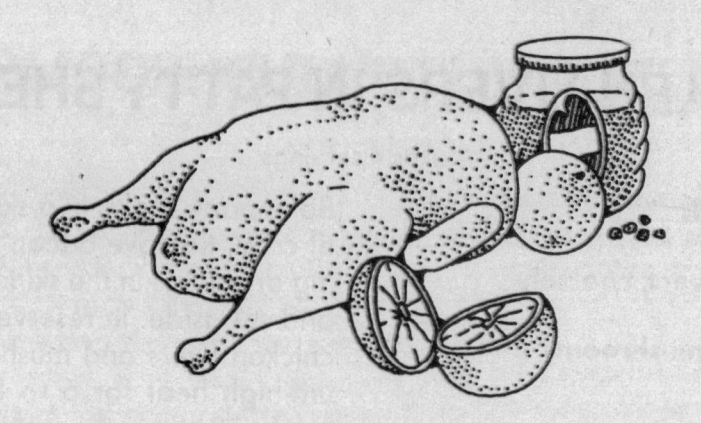

BUTTER-BROILED CHICKEN

Makes 4 servings

6 tablespoons butter or margarine, melted
¼ teaspoon seasoning salt
¼ teaspoon dried oregano, crushed
Dash garlic powder
Dash paprika
8 to 10 chicken legs or thighs

Preheat broiler. Combine butter, seasoning salt, oregano, garlic powder and paprika. Place chicken, skin-side-down, on an unheated rack of a broiler pan. Brush lightly with butter mixture. Broil 5 to 6 inches from heat for 20 minutes, brushing occasionally with butter mixture. Turn; broil for 10 minutes more or until chicken is tender, brushing occasionally.

CHICKEN AND MUSHROOMS IN TARRAGON SAUCE

Makes 4 servings

2 whole chicken breasts, skinned and boned
1½ cups sliced fresh mushrooms
2 tablespoons cooking oil
1 cup whipping cream
2 teaspoons flour
¼ teaspoon salt
¼ teaspoon crushed dried tarragon
Chicken-Flavored Rice

Cut chicken into 1-inch pieces. In a skillet, cook and stir chicken and mushrooms in hot oil over medium-high heat for 8 to 10 minutes or until tender. Drain chicken and mushrooms, discarding pan juices; keep warm. Stir together whipping cream and flour. In the same skillet, combine cream mixture, salt and tarragon. Cook and stir until thick and bubbly. Return chicken and mushrooms to skillet. Cook and stir until heated through. Serve over Chicken-Flavored Rice.

Fish

HALIBUT WITH MUSHROOMS

Makes 4 servings

- 1 pound fresh or frozen halibut, thawed or other fish steaks, cut 1 inch thick
- 1 tablespoon butter or margarine, melted
- Seasoning salt
- 1½ cups sliced fresh mushrooms
- 1 tablespoon butter or margarine
- ¼ cup whipping cream
- ¼ teaspoon dried dillweed
- Lemon wedges

Rinse fish and pat dry. Arrange in a 12 x 7½ x 2-inch baking dish. Brush with melted butter, then sprinkle with seasoning salt. Bake, uncovered, at 450° for 8 to 12 minutes or until fish flakes easily when tested with a fork. In a skillet, sauté mushrooms in 1 tablespoon hot butter over medium-high heat for 3 minutes. Stir in cream and dillweed. Bring to a boil. Reduce heat and simmer, uncovered, for 3 to 4 minutes or until slightly thickened. Serve over fish; garnish with lemon wedges.

BROILED SHRIMP KEBABS

Makes 4 servings

- 1 pound fresh or frozen large shrimp in shells, thawed
- ¼ cup cooking oil
- 4 lemon slices
- 4 whole allspice
- 3 garlic cloves, minced
- 1 teaspoon crushed dried tarragon
- 1 teaspoon crushed dried oregano
- Bay leaves, optional

Peel and devein shrimp, leaving the tail intact, if desired. In a shallow dish, combine oil, lemon, allspice, garlic, tarragon and oregano. Add shrimp. Cover and marinate for 1 hour at room temperature, stirring occasionally. (Or, marinate overnight in the refrigerator.) Preheat broiler. Drain shrimp, reserving marinade; discard lemon and allspice. Thread shrimp on short skewers alternately with bay leaves, if desired. Place on unheated rack of broiler pan. Broil 4 inches from heat for 3 to 4 minutes or until shrimp turn pink; turn and brush occasionally with reserved marinade.

Fish

FRIED RICE WITH SHRIMP

Makes 4 servings

3 tablespoons cooking oil
4 eggs, beaten
1 cup sliced green onion
1 medium green pepper, chopped
3 cups cooked rice
1 cup cooked shrimp, halved
1 cup frozen peas, thawed
2 teaspoons sugar
½ teaspoon salt

In a large skillet, heat 1 tablespoon of oil; add eggs. Cook over medium-low heat until set, without stirring; top should still be soft. Slip "egg sheet" onto a plate; cut into short narrow strips. Set aside. In the same skillet, cook and stir green onion and green pepper in the remaining 2 tablespoons oil over medium-high heat for 3 to 4 minutes or until tender-crisp. Add rice, shrimp, peas, sugar and salt; cook and stir for 3 minutes. Add egg strips; cook and stir until heated through.

BROILED SALMON STEAKS

Makes 4 servings

1 pound fresh or frozen salmon steaks, thawed, cut 1 inch thick
2 tablespoons butter or margarine, melted
1 tablespoon lemon juice
1 teaspoon Worcestershire sauce

Rinse fish and pat dry. Preheat broiler. Combine melted butter, lemon juice and Worcestershire in a small bowl. Arrange fish on the unheated rack of broiler pan. Brush lightly with butter mixture. Broil 4 inches from heat for 5 minutes. Turn; brush again. Broil for 4 to 6 minutes more or until fish flakes easily when tested with a fork. Brush with remaining butter mixture before serving.

Fish

OVEN-FRIED FISH

Makes 4 servings

- **1 pound fresh** or **frozen perch** or **other fish fillets, thawed, cut ½ inch thick**
- **1 beaten egg**
- **2 tablespoons milk**
- **¼ cup fine dry seasoned bread crumbs**
- **2 tablespoons yellow cornmeal**
- **2 tablespoons flour**
- **¼ teaspoon seasoned salt**
- **6 tablespoons butter** or **margarine, melted**
- **Lemon wedges**

Rinse fish and pat dry. In a shallow dish, combine egg and milk. In a second shallow dish, combine crumbs, cornmeal, flour and salt. Dip fish in egg mixture, then in crumb mixture. Place in a shallow baking pan. Drizzle fish with melted butter. Bake at 500° for 4 to 6 minutes or until fish flakes easily when tested with a fork. Serve with lemon wedges.

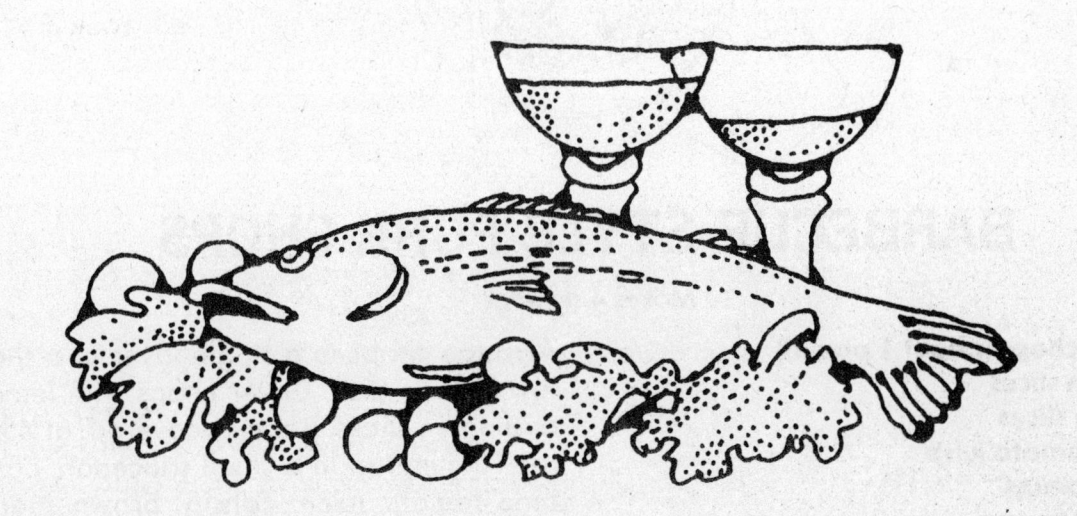

Pork

PORK CHOPS WITH BROWN RICE

Makes 4 servings

- 4 pork chops, about 1 pound
- 1 tablespoon cooking oil
- 1 package (4⅝ ounces) quick-cooking brown and wild rice mix with mushrooms
- 1⅓ cups water
- 1 stalk celery, sliced
- ½ cup sour cream

In a skillet, brown chops in hot oil over medium heat. Remove chops from the skillet; discard drippings. In the same skillet, combine rice mix, water and celery; place chops over rice mixture. Bring to a boil. Reduce heat and simmer, covered, for 30 minutes. Remove chops from the skillet; keep warm. Stir sour cream into rice mixture; heat through, but do not boil. Serve with chops.

BARBECUE-STYLE PORK CHOPS

Makes 4 servings

- 4 pork chops (about 1 pound)
- 4 lemon slices
- 4 onion slices
- ½ cup tomato juice
- ¼ cup catsup
- 1 tablespoon brown sugar
- 1 tablespoon vinegar
- 1 teaspoon Worcestershire sauce
- ¼ teaspoon chili powder

Arrange chops in a single layer in a shallow baking dish. Cover chops with lemon and onion slices. Bake, uncovered, at 450° for 10 minutes. In a small saucepan, combine tomato juice, catsup, brown sugar, vinegar, Worcestershire and chili powder. Bring to a boil. Drain chops; pour sauce over all. Reduce oven temperature to 375°. Continue baking chops, uncovered, for 40 to 45 minutes or until tender. Baste occasionally with sauce.

MOSTACCIOLI BAKE

Makes 4 servings

- 8 ounces bulk Italian sausage
- 1 cup meatless spaghetti sauce
- ½ cup cream-style cottage cheese
- ½ cup sour cream
- 1 cup shredded Mozzarella cheese
- 1 tablespoon snipped parsley
- 6 ounces mostaccioli, cooked and drained

In a skillet, brown sausage; drain. Stir in spaghetti sauce; set aside. In a bowl, combine cottage cheese, sour cream, ½ cup of Mozzarella and parsley. In a 10 x 6 x 2-inch baking dish, layer mostaccioli; spread cheese mixture over pasta. Spoon meat mixture over all. Sprinkle with remaining Mozzarella. Bake, uncovered, at 375° for 30 to 35 minutes or until heated through.

Pork

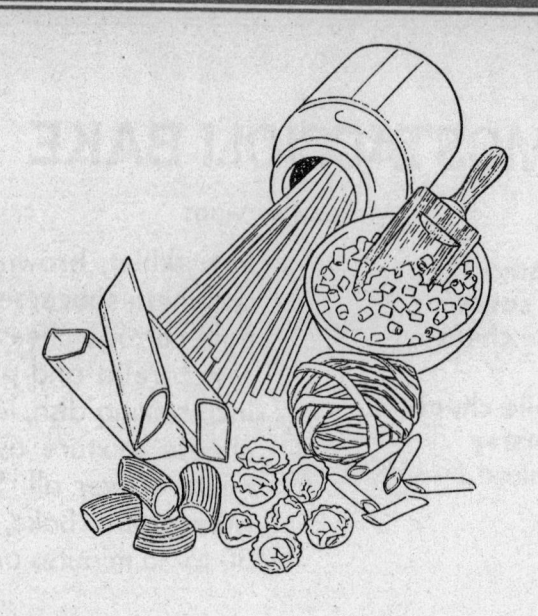

SPAGHETTI CARBONARA

Makes 4 servings

3 eggs
¾ cup light cream
½ pound bacon, cut up
12 ounces spaghetti
2 tablespoons butter or margarine
⅔ cup grated Parmesan cheese
2 tablespoons snipped parsley
Dash nutmeg

Beat eggs; blend in cream. Set aside. In a skillet, fry bacon until crisp; drain. Set aside. Cook spaghetti and drain; toss with butter until melted. Pour egg mixture over spaghetti; add bacon, Parmesan, parsley and nutmeg. Toss until well coated. Serve immediately.

BROILED HAM WITH APRICOT GLAZE

Makes 4 servings

1 1-pound fully cooked center-cut ham slice
2 tablespoons apricot preserves
1 tablespoon orange or pineapple juice
½ teaspoon Dijon-style mustard

Preheat broiler. Slash fat along edge of ham slice. Place ham on an unheated rack of a broiler pan. Broil 3 inches from heat for 3 minutes. Turn and broil for 3 minutes more. In a small bowl, combine apricot preserves, orange juice and mustard; spoon over ham. Broil for ½ to 1 minute more or until glaze is bubbly.

Rolls & Muffins

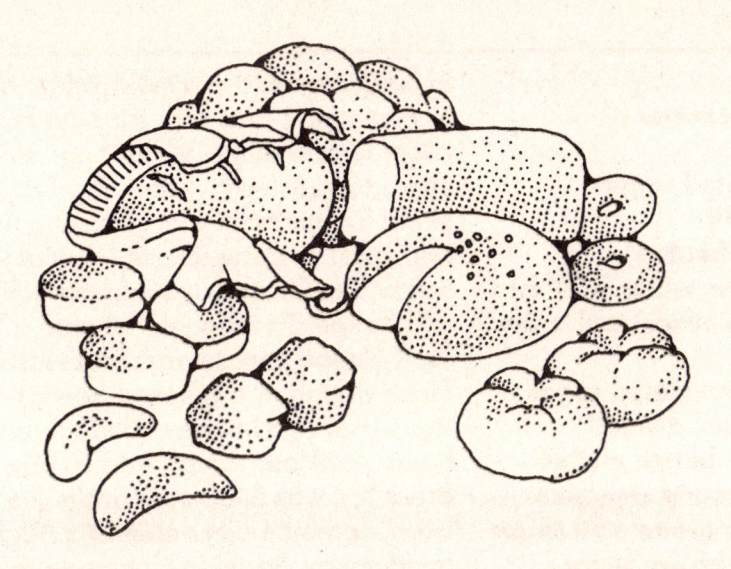

Cinnamon Rounds
Makes about 1 dozen

- 1 package active dry yeast
- ¼ cup lukewarm water
- 3 cups flour
- ¼ teaspoon salt
- 2 tablespoons sugar
- 1 cup butter *or* margarine at room temperature
- ½ cup milk, lukewarm
- 1 egg, slightly beaten
- 3 tablespoons vegetable oil
- ½ cup sugar
- ½ cup firmly packed brown sugar
- 2 tablespoons ground cinnamon

Sprinkle yeast over water; set aside. In a large bowl, mix flour, salt, and 2 tablespoons sugar. Cut in butter with a pastry blender or 2 knives; set aside. In another bowl, blend milk, egg, and oil; stir in yeast mixture. pour milk mixture over flour; stir only until all ingredients are moistened. Cover and chill for 1 hour. Turn out dough onto a lightly floured board; knead 4 or 5 times. Roll out dough to form an 11" x 8" rectangle. In a small bowl, mix remaining sugars and cinnamon. Sprinkle ½ of the mixture over dough. Roll up the dough tightly, beginning on a long side. Pinch edges to seal. Wrap in plastic wrap; chill for 1 hour. Cut dough into ½-inch slices. Sprinkle both sides of each slice with remaining sugar mixture. Flatten each slice into a 5-inch circle. Sprinkle with more sugar if dough is sticky. Place dough circles on a 10 x 15-inch non-stick cookie sheet. Bake in a preheated 400° F. oven for 10 to 12 minutes or until lightly browned. Place on wire rack to cool.

Rolls & Muffins

Pecan Rolls
Makes 1 dozen

- ½ cup milk
- 4 tablespoons butter *or* margarine
- ⅓ cup granulated sugar
- ½ teaspoon salt
- 1 egg, lightly beaten
- ¼ cup lukewarm water (110° F.)
- 1 package (¼ ounce) active dry yeast
- 1 teaspoon granulated sugar
- 2½ to 3 cups flour, divided
- 3 tablespoons butter, melted
- 1 teaspoon ground cinnamon
- 6 tablespoons granulated sugar
- ½ cup packed brown sugar
- 1 cup chopped pecans

In a saucepan, scald milk. Add 4 tablespoons butter, ⅓ cup sugar, and salt; stir until butter melts. Cool to room temperature. Stir in egg; set aside. In a bowl, sprinkle yeast and 1 teaspoon sugar over water; let stand 5 minutes. In a large mixing bowl, combine milk and yeast mixtures. Stir in 1 cup of the flour to make a soft batter. Gradually stir in remaining flour to make a stiff dough. Turn dough out onto a lightly floured surface. Knead until smooth and elastic, 8 to 10 minutes. Place dough in a greased bowl; turn once to grease top. Cover and let rise until doubled in bulk, about 1½ hours. Roll out dough into a 16 x 8-inch rectangle. Brush top with 3 tablespoons melted butter. In a small bowl, combine cinnamon and 6 tablespoons granulated sugar. Sprinkle cinnamon mixture over dough. Roll up tightly from the long side. Cut into 12 pieces. Generously grease a 12-cup muffin tin. Sprinkle ½ cup brown sugar in muffin cups. Divide pecans among muffin cups. Place a piece of dough, cut side down, in each muffin cup. Cover and let rise 30 minutes. Preheat oven to 375° F. Bake 15 minutes or until golden. Turn out rolls onto a wire rack to cool.

PARMESAN-PARSLEY ROLLS
Makes 8 rolls

- ¼ cup butter *or* margarine, softened
- 2 tablespoons grated Parmesan cheese
- 1 tablespoon snipped parsley
- 1 package refrigerated crescent rolls

Combine butter, Parmesan and parsley. Unroll crescent dough and separate into 8 triangles. Spread triangles with butter mixture. Roll up and bake.

Rolls & Muffins

Bran Muffins
Makes 6 dozen

- 2 cups boiling water
- 2 cups bran
- 2½ cups sugar
- 1 cup vegetable shortening
- 4 eggs, lightly beaten
- 1 quart buttermilk
- 5 cups flour
- 5 teaspoons baking soda
- ½ teaspoon salt
- 4 cups coarsely crushed bran cereal

In a bowl, pour boiling water over bran; let stand 5 minutes. In a mixing bowl, cream sugar and shortening until light and fluffy. Add eggs, buttermilk, and bran mixture; blend well. In a separate bowl, combine flour, baking soda, salt, and bran cereal. Gradually add to liquid mixture, blending well after each addition. Fill greased muffin cups about ⅔ full with batter. Bake at 400° F. 15 to 20 minutes or until golden. Can be stored in refrigerator up to 5 weeks.

Cranberry Orange Muffins
Makes about 1 dozen

- 2 cups flour
- ½ teaspoon salt
- 1½ teaspoons baking powder
- ½ teaspoon baking soda
- ¼ cup sugar
- ⅔ cup boiling water
- 2 tablespoons butter *or* margarine
- 1 egg, lightly beaten
- 1 cup cranberry relish
- 1 tablespoon grated orange peel

Into a large bowl, sift together flour, salt, baking powder, baking soda, and sugar; set aside. Stir butter into boiling water. Cool to room temperature. Stir egg into water. Gradually add liquids to dry ingredients; blend well. Stir in cranberry relish and orange peel. Fill greased muffin cups ⅔ full with batter. Bake at 425° F. 40 to 45 minutes or until golden.

Rolls & Muffins

Oatmeal Muffins
Makes 1 dozen

- 1½ cups flour
- ¼ cup sugar
- 4 teaspoons baking powder
- ½ teaspoon salt
- ¾ cups oatmeal
- 1 egg beaten
- 1 cup milk
- 3 tablespoons melted shortening
- ½ cup raisins

In a large bowl, mix and sift flour, sugar, baking powder, and salt. Add remaining ingredients; beat well. Fill greased muffin tins about ⅔ full. Bake in a preheated 400° F. oven 15 to 20 minutes.

Banana Muffins
Makes 1 dozen

- 2 cups sifted all-purpose flour
- ⅓ cup sugar
- 2 teaspoons baking powder
- 1½ teaspoons cinnamon
- 1 teaspoon salt
- 1 cup milk
- 1 cup mashed ripe bananas
- 1 egg, beaten
- ¼ cup melted shortening
- 1 tablespoon sugar
- ¼ teaspoon cinnamon

Into a bowl, sift flour, sugar, baking powder, cinnamon, and salt; set aside. In another bowl, combine milk, bananas, egg, and shortening; add all at once to flour mixture, stirring only until dry ingredients are moistened. The batter will be lumpy. Fill greased muffin tins ⅔ full. Mix together remaining 1 tablespoon sugar and ¼ teaspoon cinnamon; sprinkle on top of each muffin. Bake in a preheated 400° F. oven for 25 minutes.

Rolls & Muffins

Poppy Seed Muffins
Makes about 1½ dozen

- ¾ cup sugar
- ¼ cup butter *or* margarine, softened
- ½ teaspoon grated orange peel
- 2 eggs
- 2 cup flour
- 2½ teaspoons baking powder
- ½ teaspoon salt
- ¼ teaspoon ground nutmeg
- 1 cup milk
- ½ cup golden raisins
- ½ cup chopped pecans
- ¼ cup poppy seed

In a large mixing bowl, cream sugar, butter, and orange peel until light and fluffy. Add eggs, one at a time, beating well after each addition. In a separate bowl, combine flour, baking powder, salt, and nutmeg. Alternately add flour mixture and milk to creamed mixture; blend well after each addition. Stir in raisins, nuts, and poppy seed. Fill greased muffin cups ¾ full with batter. Bake at 400° F. 20 minutes or until golden.

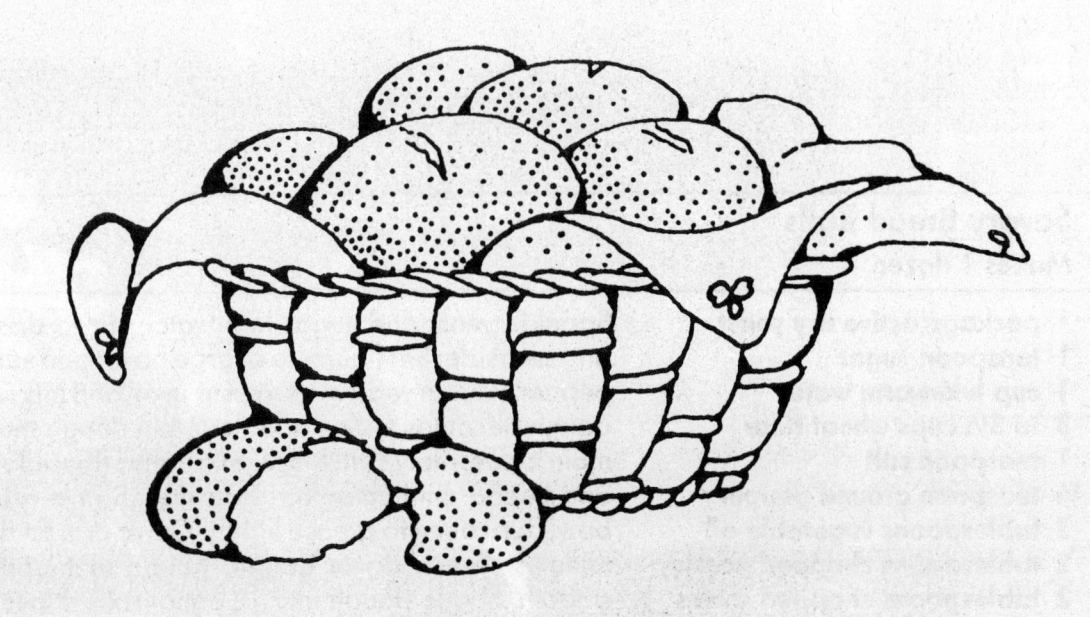

Rolls & Muffins

Breakfast Rolls
Makes 1 dozen

- ¾ cup milk, lukewarm
- 1 package active dry yeast
- 2 teaspoons sugar
- 3½ to 4 cups flour
- ¾ cup sugar
- ¼ teaspoon salt
- ¼ cup butter *or* margarine, melted and cooled to lukewarm
- 1 egg, beaten
- 1 teaspoon vanilla
- 2 tablespoons butter *or* margarine

Pour lukewarm milk into a small bowl. Stir in yeast and 2 teaspoons sugar; set aside. Into a large bowl, sift flour. Make a hollow in the center and add ¾ cup sugar, salt, melted butter, egg, vanilla, and yeast mixture; mix well. If the dough becomes sticky, add flour, but dough must remain moderately soft. Place dough on a lightly floured board and knead until smooth. Place in a greased bowl; turn once to grease lightly. Cover and let rise 1½ hours or until doubled in bulk. Punch down dough. Turn out onto a lightly floured board and knead until smooth. Form dough into 12 equal balls. Melt remaining 2 tablespoons butter in a pie plate. Roll the dough balls in the butter; cover and let rise 25 minutes or until doubled in bulk. Bake in a preheated 400° F. oven for 25 to 30 minutes or until rolls are golden brown and sound hollow when bottom is tapped. Remove and cool on wire rack.

Savory Bread Rolls
Makes 1 dozen

- 1 package active dry yeast
- 1 teaspoon sugar
- 1 cup lukewarm water
- 3 to 3½ cups wheat flour
- 1 teaspoon salt
- ⅛ teaspoon ground pepper
- 3 tablespoons vegetable oil
- 2 tablespoons chopped parsley
- 2 tablespoons chopped chives
- 1 teaspoon chopped dill
- 1 egg yolk
- 1 teaspoon water

Sprinkle yeast and sugar into water, stir to dissolve, and set aside. Sift flour into a large bowl; add salt and pepper. Pour in yeast mixture; stir in oil and mix well. If dough becomes sticky, add flour, but dough must remain moderately soft. Place on a lightly floured board and knead until smooth. Place dough in a greased bowl; turn once to grease lightly. Cover and let rise 45 minutes. Punch down dough. Knead in herbs until smooth. Shape dough into 12 equal rolls. Place on a greased 10 x 15-inch cookie sheet. Cover and let rise 45 minutes or until doubled in bulk. Cut two ¼-inch deep slashes in the top of each roll, forming a cross. Combine egg yolk and water. Brush tops of rolls with mixture. Bake in a preheated 350° F. oven for 25 minutes or until rolls are golden brown and sound hollow when tapped.

Sauces, Dips & Dressings

TARTAR SAUCE

Makes about 1 cup

¾ cup mayonnaise or salad dressing
3 tablespoons finely chopped onion
3 tablespoons pickle relish

Combine mayonnaise, onion and pickle relish; cover and chill until serving time.

CHOCOLATE-PEANUT SAUCE

Makes about 1½ cups

¾ cup milk
⅓ cup sugar
2 squares semi-sweet chocolate
½ cup chunk-style peanut butter
Vanilla ice cream

In a saucepan, combine milk, sugar and chocolate. Bring to a boil, stirring constantly. Remove from heat. Using a whisk, blend in peanut butter. Stir occasionally as sauce cools. (Sauce will thicken as it cools.) Serve warm or cold over ice cream. If sauce is too thick when cold, stir in a little water.

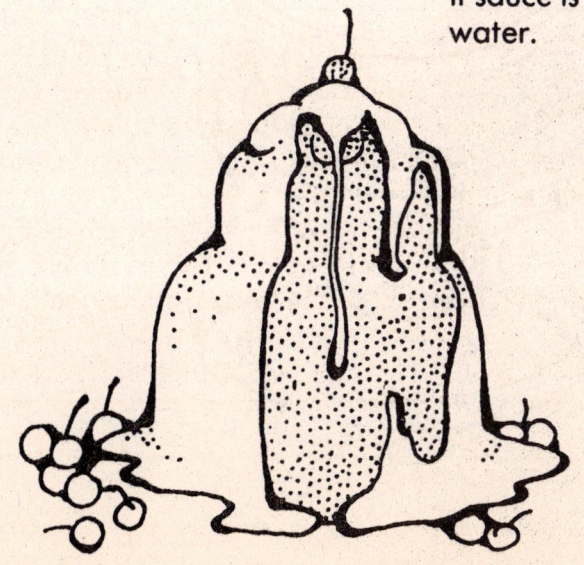

Sauces, Dips & Dressings

HOT BUTTER-PECAN SAUCE

Makes about ½ cup

¼ cup finely chopped pecans
¼ cup butter *or* margarine
½ cup sugar
¼ cup water
½ teaspoon vanilla
Vanilla ice cream

In a small saucepan, cook pecans in butter over medium heat until golden. Stir in sugar and water. Bring to a boil. Reduce heat and simmer, uncovered, about 5 minutes or until slightly thickened, stirring often. Remove from heat; stir in vanilla. Serve warm over ice cream.

AVOCADO DIP

Makes about 1 cup

1 avocado, peeled and seeded
⅓ cup sour cream
2 tablespoons Italian salad dressing
1 teaspoon lemon juice
Dash garlic salt
1 to 2 tablespoons milk

In a bowl, mash avocado, using a fork. Stir in sour cream, salad dressing, lemon juice and garlic salt; add milk until of dipping consistency. Serve with crisp relishes.

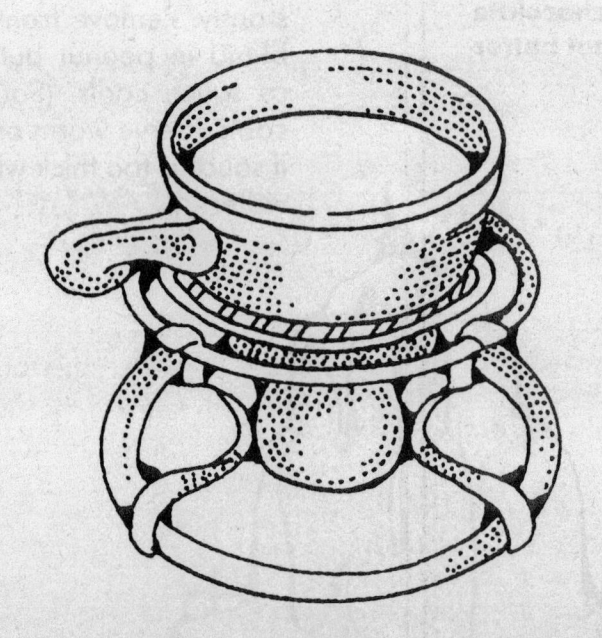

Sauces, Dips & Dressings

DILL DIP
Makes 1 cup

¾ cup sour cream
¼ cup mayonnaise or salad dressing
1 tablespoon instant minced onion
1 teaspoon dried dillweed
1 teaspoon dried parsley flakes
¼ teaspoon seasoning salt

In a bowl, combine sour cream, mayonnaise, onion, dillweed, parsley and salt; cover and chill. Serve with crisp relishes.

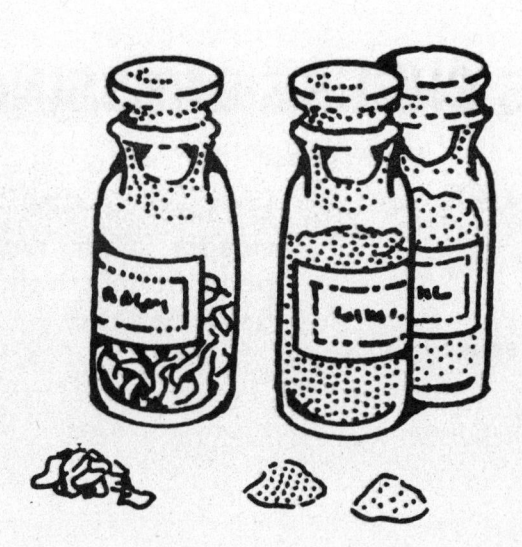

TARRAGON-OIL DRESSING
Makes about ¾ cup

½ cup olive or salad oil
3 tablespoons tarragon vinegar
2 tablespoons lemon juice
1 teaspoon Dijon-style mustard
1 clove garlic, minced
⅛ teaspoon salt
 Dash pepper
 Fresh greens

In a screw-top jar, combine oil, vinegar, lemon juice, mustard, garlic, salt and pepper. Cover and shake thoroughly. Chill. Shake again before serving over fresh greens.

Sauces, Dips & Dressings

HONEY-FRENCH DRESSING

Makes 1 cup

⅓ cup vinegar
⅓ cup catsup
⅓ cup honey
1 onion slice
½ teaspoon celery seed
¼ teaspoon dry mustard
⅓ cup salad oil
Fresh greens

In a blender container, combine vinegar, catsup, honey, onion, celery seed and dry mustard; cover and blend until smooth. With blender running, gradually add oil. Cover and chill. Serve with fresh greens.

BLUE CHEESE DRESSING

Makes about 1 cup

¾ cup sour cream
¼ cup buttermilk
1 tablespoon vinegar
1 teaspoon sugar
½ teaspoon Worcestershire sauce
Dash garlic powder
¼ cup crumbled blue cheese

In a bowl, combine sour cream, buttermilk, vinegar, sugar, Worcestershire and garlic powder; mix well. Stir in blue cheese. Cover and chill.

Sauces, Dips & Dressings

MELON IN CITRUS SAUCE

Makes 4 servings

¼ cup sugar
¼ cup orange juice
3 tablespoons lime juice
2 cups cubed honeydew melon
2 cups cubed cantaloupe

In a bowl, combine sugar, orange juice and lime juice; stir until sugar dissolves. Add honeydew and cantaloupe; stir gently. Cover and chill. Stir again before serving.

BLUEBERRY SAUCE

Makes 1 cup

1 cup fresh or frozen blueberries, thawed
3 tablespoons sugar
2 teaspoons cornstarch
½ cup water
1 teaspoon lemon juice

In a saucepan, crush ⅓ cup of the blueberries. Combine sugar and cornstarch; stir in water. Add sugar mixture to saucepan. Cook and stir over medium heat until thick and bubbly. Cook and stir 2 minutes more. Remove from heat; stir in remaining ⅔ cup blueberries and lemon juice. Cool. Serve over sherbet.

Soups & Salads

CLAM CHOWDER

Makes 4 servings

- 1 can (6½ ounces) minced clams
- 2 slices bacon
- 3 cups frozen hash brown potatoes with onion and peppers
- 2 cups light cream
- 1 cup milk
- ¾ teaspoon garlic salt
- Dash pepper
- 2 tablespoons flour

Drain clams, reserving juice. Add water to reserved juice to equal 1 cup; set aside. In a medium saucepan, fry bacon until crisp; drain and crumble. Set aside. Discard bacon drippings. In the same saucepan, combine hash browns and reserved clam juice mixture. Bring to a boil. Reduce heat and simmer, covered, about 8 minutes or until vegetables are tender. Stir in clams, light cream, ¾ cup of milk, salt and pepper. Blend remaining ¼ cup milk and flour; stir into clam mixture. Cook and stir over medium heat until thick and bubbly. Cook and stir for 1 minute more.

Soups & Salads

SWISS CHEESE SOUP

Makes 4 servings

3 tablespoons butter *or* margarine
¼ cup flour
1 teaspoon instant chicken bouillon granules
¼ teaspoon paprika
3½ cups milk
6 slices processed Swiss cheese
1 teaspoon snipped chives

Melt butter in a medium saucepan. Stir in flour, bouillon granules and paprika. Cook and stir over medium heat until bubbly. Add milk all at once. Cook and stir until thick and bubbly; cook and stir 1 minute more. Stir in cheese and chives. Stir over low heat until cheese melts.

CHEESY CHICKEN AND NOODLES

Makes 4 servings

3 cups water
2 teaspoons instant chicken bouillon granules
½ teaspoon salt
6 ounces medium noodles
½ cup sour cream
1 tablespoon flour
2 cups diced cooked chicken
½ of an 8-ounce jar cheese spread
1 teaspoon snipped parsley

In a medium saucepan, bring water, bouillon granules and salt to a boil; stir in noodles. Return to a boil; reduce heat and simmer, uncovered, for 10 minutes, stirring occasionally. In a bowl, stir together sour cream and flour. Stir chicken, cheese spread, parsley and sour cream mixture into undrained noodles. Cook and stir until thick and bubbly. Cook and stir 1 minute more.

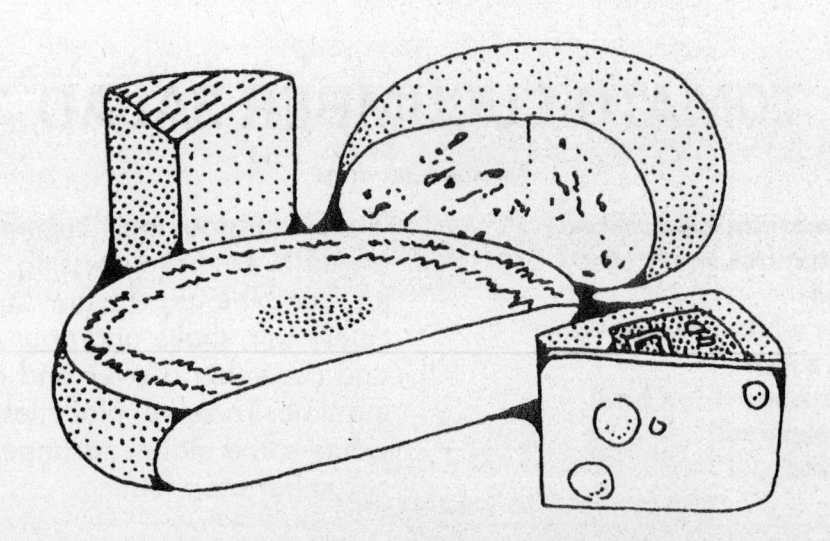

Soups & Salads

MIXED VEGETABLE SALAD

Makes 4 servings

1 box (10 ounces) frozen mixed vegetables
½ cup Green Goddess salad dressing
½ cup halved cherry tomatoes
2 tablespoons sliced pitted ripe olives
Lettuce leaves

Cook vegetables; rinse under cold water and drain thoroughly. Pour dressing over vegetables; cover and chill at least 30 minutes. Stir in tomatoes and ripe olives. Serve on lettuce leaves.

TOMATO-CUCUMBER SALAD

Makes 6 servings

3 medium tomatoes, thinly sliced
1 medium cucumber, thinly sliced
⅓ cup salad oil
3 tablespoons white wine vinegar
1 tablespoon sugar
½ teaspoon crushed dried basil
¼ teaspoon celery salt
Lettuce leaves

Place tomatoes and cucumber in a shallow dish. To make dressing, in a screw-top jar, combine oil, vinegar, sugar, basil and celery salt; shake and pour over tomatoes and cucumber. Cover and chill until serving time. To serve, place lettuce on 6 individual salad plates. Arrange tomatoes and cucumber atop lettuce.

Soups & Salads

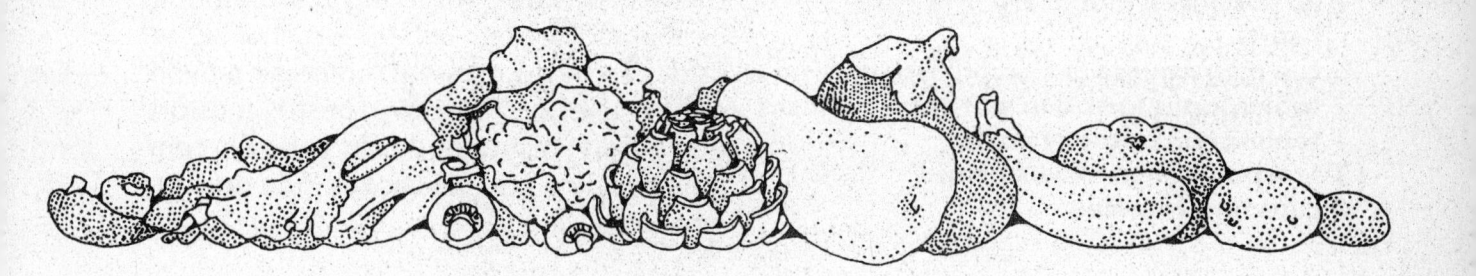

MIXED GREEN SALAD

Makes 4 servings

2 cups torn leaf lettuce
2 cups torn romaine lettuce
1 cup broccoli florets
1 small zucchini, thinly sliced
4 radishes, sliced
2 green onions, sliced
Blue Cheese Dressing

In a salad bowl, combine lettuce, romaine, broccoli, zucchini, radishes and green onion. Just before serving, toss with some of the Blue Cheese Dressing.

BOSTON LETTUCE SALAD

Makes 4 servings

½ cup sour cream
¼ cup Italian salad dressing
2 tablespoons mayonnaise *or* salad dressing
1 teaspoon snipped parsley
2 small heads Boston lettuce
¼ cup shredded Cheddar cheese

To make dressing, in a screw-top jar, combine sour cream, salad dressing, mayonnaise and parsley. Core lettuce; cut each head in half. Arrange lettuce on salad plates; top with dressing. Sprinkle with cheese.

Soups & Salads

ROMAINE AND ARTICHOKE TOSS

Makes 4 servings

- 1 jar (6 ounces) marinated artichoke hearts
- ¼ cup mayonnaise or salad dressing
- 2 tablespoons tarragon vinegar
- 1 tablespoon anchovy paste
- 1 teaspoon Dijon-style mustard
- 3 cups torn romaine

Drain artichokes, reserving 2 tablespoons of the marinade. Cut up artichokes; set aside. To make dressing, combine mayonnaise, vinegar, anchovy paste, mustard and reserved marinade. In a bowl, combine romaine and artichokes; add dressing and toss.

ITALIAN SALAD

Makes 4 servings

- ¼ cup tarragon vinegar
- 1 tablespoon mayonnaise or salad dressing
- 1 teaspoon Dijon-style mustard
- ½ teaspoon crushed dried oregano
- Dash garlic powder
- ½ cup olive or salad oil
- 4 cups torn romaine
- ¼ cup grated Parmesan cheese
- ¼ cup seasoned croutons

To make dressing, in a screw-top jar, combine vinegar, mayonnaise, mustard, oregano and garlic powder. Using a whisk, slowly blend in oil, beating constantly. In a salad bowl, combine romaine, Parmesan and croutons; pour dressing over all and toss.

Soups & Salads

AVOCADO-ORANGE SALAD

Makes 4 servings

Bibb lettuce
2 oranges, peeled and sliced
1 avocado, seeded, peeled and sliced
1 small onion, sliced and separated into rings
½ cup clear French salad dressing

Line 4 salad plates with lettuce; arrange oranges, avocado and onion atop lettuce. Drizzle with salad dressing.

FRUIT AND YOGURT SALAD

Makes 4 servings

Leaf lettuce
2 medium apples, chopped
1 cup seedless green grapes, halved
½ cup mandarin orange sections
¼ cup flaked coconut
½ cup strawberry yogurt

Line individual salad plates with leaf lettuce. Combine apples, grapes, mandarin oranges and flaked coconut; toss lightly. Spoon fruit mixture onto lettuce-lined plates. Drizzle strawberry yogurt over fruit.

Soups & Salads

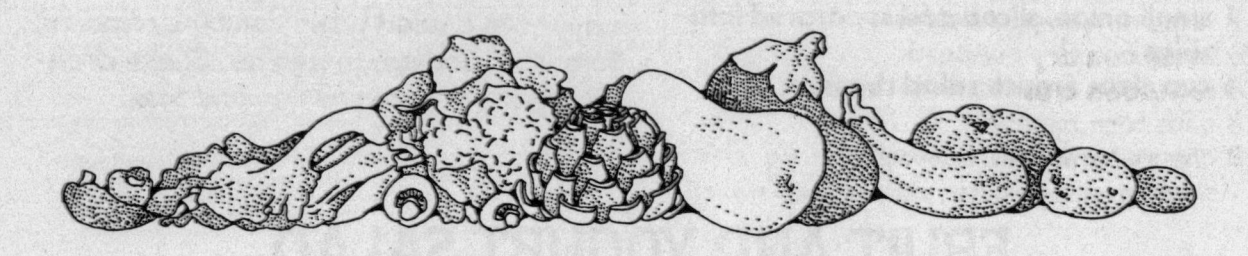

GREEN SALAD TOSS

Makes 6 servings

4 cups torn lettuce
2 cups torn curly endive
½ medium green pepper, sliced
2 cups cauliflower florets
⅓ cup olive or salad oil
3 tablespoons vinegar
Dash garlic powder
Dash salt
Freshly ground black pepper

In a salad bowl, combine lettuce, endive, green pepper and cauliflower. For dressing, in a screw-top jar, combine oil, vinegar, garlic powder, salt and pepper; shake thoroughly. Pour dressing over salad; toss lightly.

TUNA-SHOESTRING SALAD

Makes 4 servings

1 can (9¼ ounces) tuna
2 stalks celery, chopped
2 carrots, shredded
½ small onion, chopped
8 pitted ripe olives, sliced
¾ cup mayonnaise or salad dressing
1 teaspoon lemon juice
1 teaspoon prepared mustard
1½ cups shoestring potatoes
Lettuce leaves

Drain tuna; break into chunks. In a medium bowl, combine tuna, celery, carrots, onion and olives; set aside. To make dressing, combine mayonnaise, lemon juice and mustard. Add to tuna mixture; toss. Cover and chill. Just before serving, add shoestring potatoes. Toss together. Serve on lettuce leaves.

Soups & Salads

VINAIGRETTE SALAD

Makes 4 servings

1/3 cup salad oil
1/4 cup white wine vinegar
2 teaspoons sugar
1 teaspoon snipped chives
1/2 teaspoon dry mustard
1/2 teaspoon crushed dried basil
3 cups torn romaine
8 cherry tomatoes, halved
1 small green pepper, coarsely chopped

To make dressing, in a screw-top jar, combine oil, vinegar, sugar, chives, dry mustard and basil; cover and shake thoroughly. In a salad bowl, combine romaine, tomatoes and green pepper. Shake dressing again; pour over salad and toss.

COLESLAW

Makes 4 servings

2 cups shredded cabbage
1/4 cup shredded carrot
1 tablespoon finely chopped onion
1/3 cup dairy sour cream
2 tablespoons sugar
2 tablespoons vinegar
1/8 teaspoon salt
Dash garlic powder

In a bowl, combine cabbage, carrot and onion; set aside. To make dressing, in a screw-top jar, combine sour cream, sugar, vinegar, salt and garlic powder; shake until sugar dissolves. Pour over cabbage mixture; toss. Cover and chill. Toss again before serving.

Soups & Salads

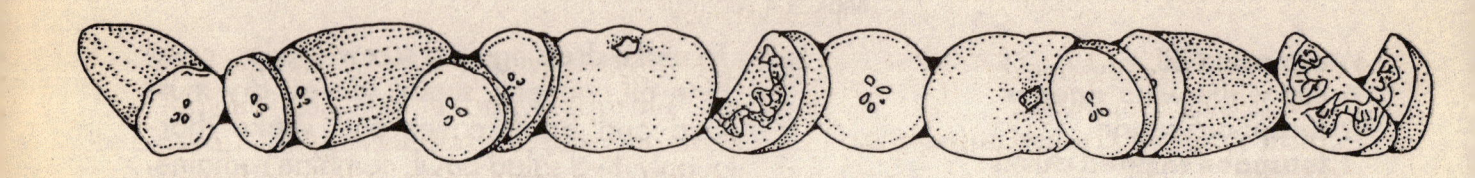

CUCUMBER-PEA SALAD

Makes 4 servings

- 1 cup frozen peas
- ⅓ cup salad oil
- 2 tablespoons vinegar
- 1 teaspoon sugar
- ¼ teaspoon dry mustard
- ¼ teaspoon paprika
- ¼ teaspoon dried tarragon, crushed
- 3 cups torn lettuce
- 1 small cucumber, peeled and chopped
- ½ of a 3-ounce can French-fried onions, coarsely crushed

Pour boiling water over frozen peas; let stand for 2 minutes. Drain thoroughly. For dressing, in a screw-top jar, combine oil, vinegar, sugar, dry mustard, paprika and tarragon. Cover and shake thoroughly. In a salad bowl, combine lettuce, cucumber and peas; toss with dressing. Sprinkle with French-fried onions.

SPINACH-BACON TOSS

Makes 4 servings

- ½ cup salad oil
- ⅓ cup sugar
- 1 small onion, quartered
- 3 tablespoons vinegar
- 2 teaspoons prepared mustard
- ½ teaspoon celery seed
- 6 slices bacon
- 6 cups torn spinach
- 1 cup sliced fresh mushrooms
- 2 hard-boiled eggs, chopped

To make dressing, in a blender container, combine oil, sugar, onion, vinegar, mustard and celery seed. Cover and blend until smooth. Cover and chill. In a skillet, fry bacon until crisp; drain and crumble. In a large salad bowl, combine spinach, mushrooms, eggs and bacon; pour dressing over salad. Toss lightly.

Soups & Salads

CHICKEN SALAD IN CROISSANTS

Makes 4 servings

- 2 cups diced cooked chicken
- 1 stalk celery, chopped
- 1 can (8¼ ounces) crushed pineapple, drained
- 2 tablespoons sliced pimiento-stuffed olives
- ½ cup mayonnaise *or* salad dressing
- Dash salt
- Leaf lettuce
- 4 croissants, split
- ¼ cup chopped cashews

In a medium bowl, combine chicken, celery, pineapple and olives. Add mayonnaise and salt; toss together lightly. Cover and chill. To serve, place a lettuce leaf in each croissant. Spoon chicken salad over lettuce; sprinkle with cashews.

TACO SALAD

Makes 4 servings

- 1 pound ground beef
- 1 small onion, chopped
- ½ cup taco sauce
- ½ cup sour cream
- ¼ teaspoon salt
- 4 cups shredded lettuce
- ¾ cup shredded Cheddar cheese
- 2 medium tomatoes, chopped
- Sliced pitted ripe olives
- Tortilla chips

In a medium skillet, cook and stir ground beef and onion over medium-high heat until meat is brown and onion is tender. Drain thoroughly. In a bowl, combine meat mixture, taco sauce, half of the sour cream and salt. Cover and chill for 20 to 30 minutes. To serve, place lettuce on 4 individual salad plates. Sprinkle with cheese and tomatoes. Spoon meat mixture over salads. Top with remaining sour cream and garnish with olive slices. Serve with tortilla chips.

Soups & Salads

JAMBALAYA
Makes 4 or 5 servings

- 1 cup cubed fully cooked ham
- 2 green onions, chopped
- 1 tablespoon butter *or* margarine
- 1 can (28 ounces) tomatoes, undrained
- 1 cup water
- ¾ cup long-grain rice
- 1 bay leaf
- 1 teaspoon instant beef bouillon granules
- ½ teaspoon sugar
- Dash hot pepper sauce
- 1 cup cooked shrimp, halved
- 1 medium green pepper, cut into 1-inch squares

In a large saucepan, cook and stir ham and green onions in hot butter over medium-high heat for 3 to 4 minutes or until onions are tender. Stir in tomatoes, water, rice, bay leaf, bouillon granules, sugar and hot pepper sauce. Bring to a boil. Reduce heat and simmer, covered, about 15 minutes or until rice is tender. Stir in shrimp and green pepper. Simmer, uncovered, for 6 to 8 minutes or until of desired consistency. Remove bay leaf before serving.

MINESTRONE WITH SAUSAGE
Makes 6 servings

- 8 ounces bulk Italian sausage
- 1 small onion, chopped
- 1 carrot, chopped
- 2 cups water
- 1 can (16 ounces) tomatoes, undrained
- 1 can (15 ounces) Great Northern beans, drained
- 2 teaspoons instant beef bouillon granules
- 1 teaspoon salt
- ½ teaspoon crushed dried basil
- Dash garlic powder
- ¾ cup small shell macaroni
- 1 small zucchini, chopped
- Grated Parmesan cheese

In a Dutch oven, cook sausage, onion and carrot over medium-high heat until meat is brown and vegetables are tender, stirring occasionally; drain. Add water, tomatoes, beans, bouillon granules, salt, basil and garlic powder. Bring to a boil. Reduce heat and simmer, covered, for 20 minutes. Stir in macaroni; simmer, covered, for 5 minutes. Stir in zucchini; simmer, uncovered, about 5 minutes or until zucchini and macaroni are tender, stirring occasionally. Serve with Parmesan.

Vegetables & Rice

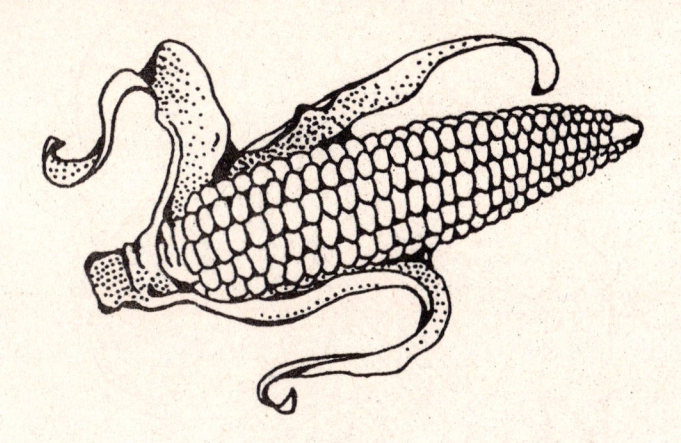

CORN WITH MUSHROOMS

Makes 4 servings

- 1 package (10 ounces) frozen whole kernel corn
- 1 cup sliced fresh mushrooms
- 2 tablespoons butter or margarine
- 1 tablespoon snipped parsley

Cook and drain corn. In a skillet, cook and stir mushrooms in hot butter over medium-high heat for 3 to 4 minutes or until tender. Stir in corn and parsley.

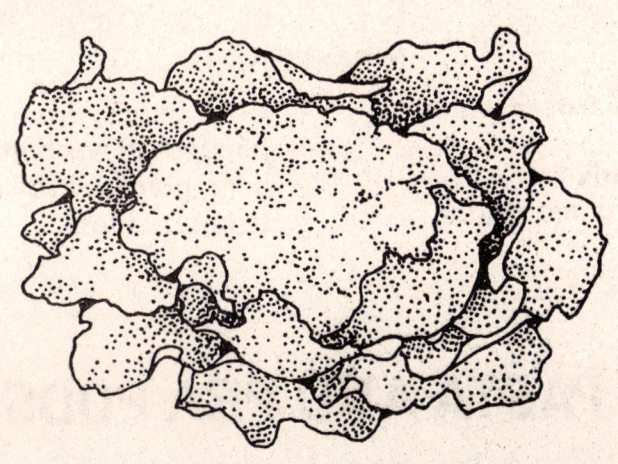

CAULIFLOWER WITH ALMOND-DILL BUTTER

Makes 4 servings

- 1 package (10 ounces) frozen cauliflower
- 2 tablespoons slivered almonds
- 2 tablespoons butter or margarine
- ¼ teaspoon dried dillweed

Cook cauliflower; drain. In a small saucepan, cook almonds in butter over low heat until golden, stirring frequently. Stir in dill. Pour over cauliflower and toss.

Vegetables & Rice

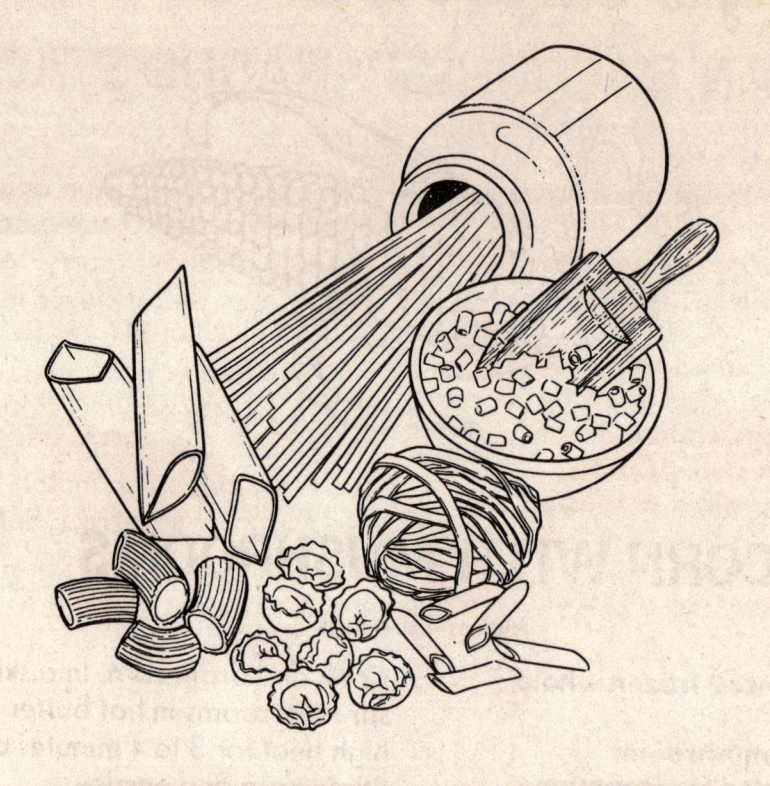

GREEN BEANS AMANDINE

Makes 4 servings

- 1 package (9 ounces) frozen whole green beans
- ¼ cup slivered almonds
- 1 tablespoon butter or margarine

Cook beans; drain. In a small skillet, sauté almonds in hot butter for 1 to 2 minutes or until golden brown. Pour almonds over beans and toss.

PASTA AND PEA PODS

Makes 4 servings

- 8 ounces mostaccioli
- 1 package (6 ounces) frozen pea pods, cooked
- ½ cup butter or margarine
  Salt
  Pepper
- ¼ cup grated Romano cheese
  Julienned carrots, optional

Cook mostaccioli and pea pods; drain and keep warm. In a skillet, melt butter over medium heat until golden brown. Remove from heat; add mostaccioli and pea pods. Toss together. Season to taste with salt and pepper. Transfer to a serving bowl; sprinkle with Romano. Garnish with julienned carrots, if desired.

Vegetables & Rice

CANADIAN BACON-ASPARAGUS STACK-UPS

Makes 4 servings

- 1 package (10 ounces) frozen asparagus spears
- 3 tablespoons butter or margarine
- 2 tablespoons flour
- ½ teaspoon salt
- ¼ teaspoon curry powder
- 1⅔ cups milk
- 2 hard-boiled eggs, chopped
- 8 slices Canadian-style bacon
- 4 English muffins, split and toasted
  Paprika

Cook asparagus; drain and keep warm. In a saucepan, melt 2 tablespoons butter. Stir in flour, salt and curry. Add milk all at once. Cook and stir over medium heat until thick and bubbly; stir in eggs. Cook and stir until heated through; keep warm. In a skillet, lightly brown Canadian bacon on both sides in remaining 1 tablespoon butter. Place bacon on muffin halves; arrange asparagus over bacon. Spoon sauce over all; sprinkle with paprika.

SEASONED ITALIAN GREEN BEANS

Makes 4 servings

- 1 package (9 ounces) frozen Italian green beans, cooked
- 2 tablespoons regular onion soup mix
- ¼ teaspoon crushed dried oregano
- 1 tablespoon chopped pimiento

Cook beans adding dry onion soup mix and oregano to water. Drain and stir in pimiento.

Vegetables & Rice

PEAS WITH CELERY

Makes 4 servings

- 1 package (10 ounces) frozen peas
- ½ cup sliced celery
- 2 tablespoons butter or margarine
- ¼ teaspoon crushed dried thyme

Cook peas; drain. In a small saucepan, cook and stir celery in hot butter over medium-high heat for 3 to 4 minutes or until tender-crisp; stir in thyme. Pour over peas and toss.

BROCCOLI WITH CASHEWS

Makes 4 servings

- 1 package (10 ounces) frozen broccoli spears
- ¼ cup coarsely chopped cashews
- 1 tablespoon butter or margarine
- 2 teaspoons finely shredded lemon rind

Cook broccoli; drain. In a small skillet, cook and stir cashews in hot butter for 1 to 2 minutes or until golden brown. Remove from heat; stir in lemon rind. Pour over broccoli spears.

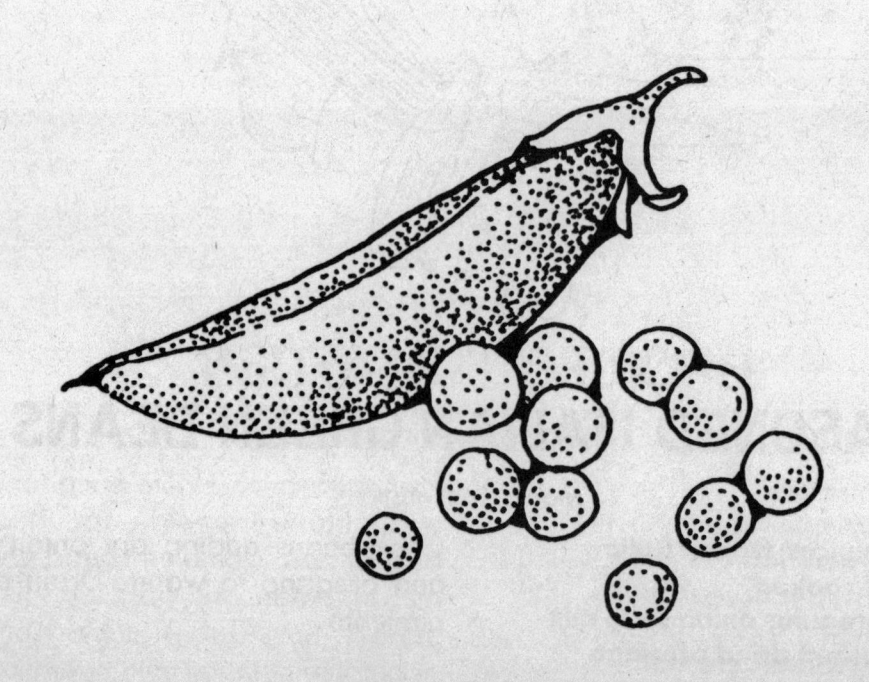

Vegetables & Rice

SAUTÉED CARROTS AND ONIONS

Makes 4 servings

1 pound carrots, cut into julienne strips
1 medium onion, sliced
2 tablespoons butter or margarine
½ teaspoon sugar
¼ teaspoon salt

In a skillet, cook carrots and onion in hot butter over medium-high heat for 8 to 10 minutes or until tender-crisp, stirring frequently. Stir in sugar and salt.

BROILED TOMATOES

Makes 4 servings

2 large ripe tomatoes
¾ cup soft bread crumbs
¼ cup grated Parmesan cheese
2 tablespoons butter or margarine, melted
¼ teaspoon dried basil, crushed

Preheat broiler. Halve each tomato crosswise. Place, cut-side-up, in a shallow baking pan. Combine bread crumbs, Parmesan, butter and basil; sprinkle over tomatoes. Broil 3 to 4 inches from the heat about 4 minutes or until lightly browned.

Vegetables & Rice

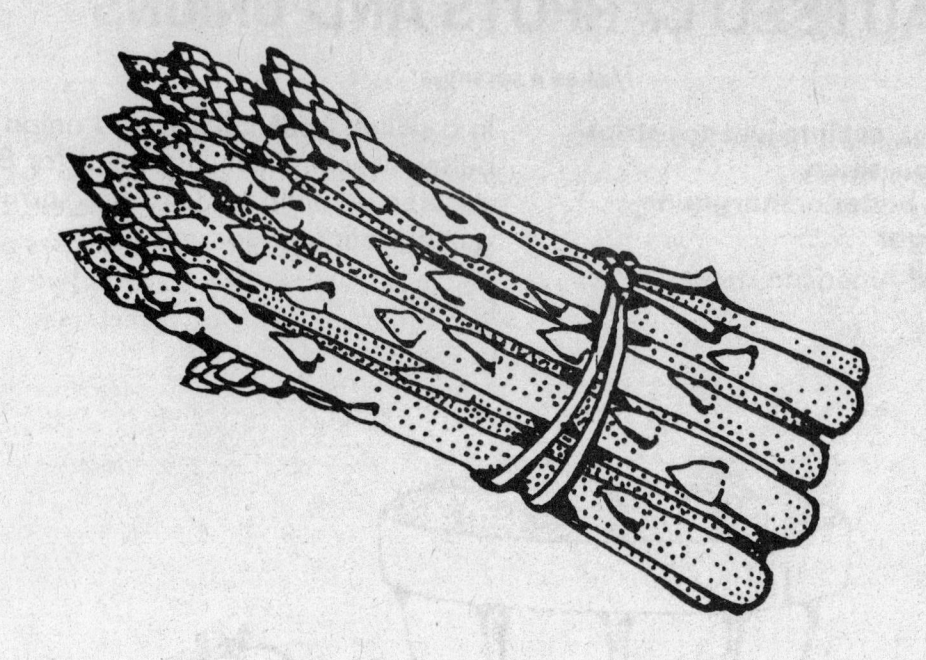

ASPARAGUS WITH SESAME SEED

Makes 6 servings

- ½ cup water
- ½ teaspoon salt
- 1½ pounds fresh asparagus, cut into 1½-inch lengths
- 2 tablespoons butter or margarine
- 1 tablespoon sesame seed, toasted
- 2 teaspoons lemon juice

In a saucepan, bring water and salt to a boil; add asparagus. Cook, covered, about 8 minutes or until tender. Drain. Stir in butter, sesame seed and lemon juice.

OVEN POTATOES WITH DILL

Makes 4 servings

- 1 pound new potatoes, unpeeled
- 3 tablespoons butter or margarine
- ½ teaspoon salt
- ½ teaspoon dried dillweed

Cut potatoes into quarters. Place in a 1½-quart casserole with butter, salt and dillweed. Bake, covered, at 425° for about 45 minutes or until tender, stirring occasionally.

Vegetables & Rice

HASH BROWNS AU GRATIN

Makes 4 servings

1 package (12 ounces) frozen loose-pack hash brown potatoes
1 cup whipping cream
½ teaspoon salt
¼ cup shredded American cheese

Arrange frozen potatoes in a 1-quart casserole. Pour whipping cream over all; sprinkle with salt. Bake, uncovered, at 375° about 45 minutes or until potatoes are tender and saucy, stirring once or twice. Sprinkle with cheese the last 5 minutes.

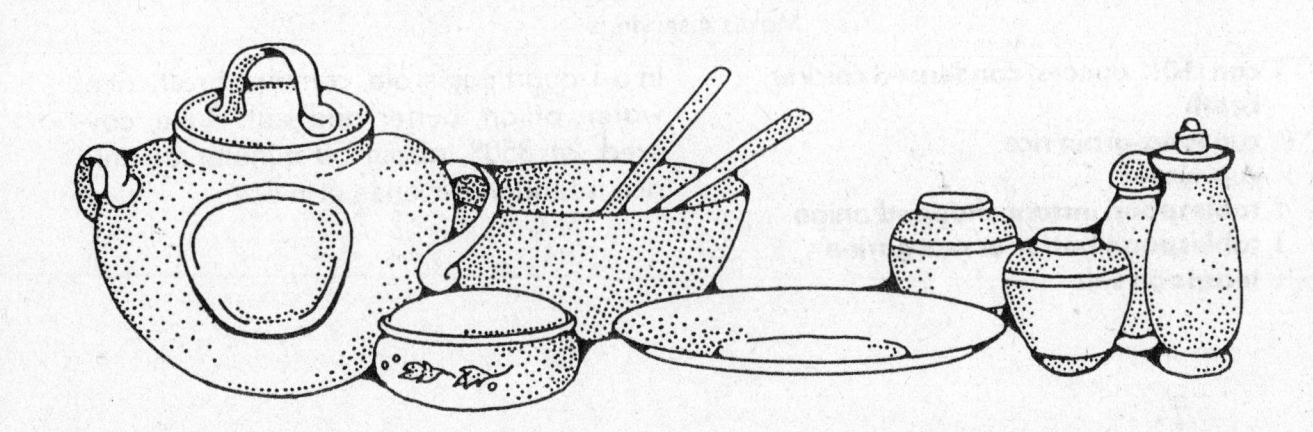

HASH BROWNS WITH CHEESE

Makes 4 servings

¼ cup cooking oil
1 package (12 ounces) frozen loose-pack hash brown potatoes
½ teaspoon salt
1 cup shredded Swiss or Cheddar cheese

In a large skillet, heat oil over medium-high heat. Add potatoes; spread into an even layer. Sprinkle with salt. Cover and cook over medium-high heat for 6 minutes; stir. Cover and cook for 3 to 4 minutes more or until golden brown. Remove from heat. Add cheese and toss; cover for 1 minute.

Vegetables & Rice

SAFFRON RICE
Makes 4 servings

1⅓ cups cold water
⅔ cup long-grain rice
2 tablespoons butter or margarine
¾ teaspoon salt
⅛ teaspoon saffron
2 tablespoons snipped parsley

In a saucepan, combine water, rice, butter, salt and saffron. Cover and bring to a boil. Reduce heat. Simmer, covered, for 15 minutes. Remove from heat. Let stand, covered, for 10 minutes. Stir in parsley.

CHICKEN-FLAVORED RICE
Makes 4 servings

1 can (10¾ ounces) condensed chicken broth
⅔ cup long-grain rice
¼ cup water
1 tablespoon instant chopped onion
1 tablespoon butter or margarine
½ teaspoon salt

In a 1-quart casserole, combine broth, rice, water, onion, butter and salt. Bake, covered, at 350°, about 50 minutes or until rice is tender; stir once or twice.

Vegetables & Rice

BROCCOLI SAUTÉ

Makes 4 servings

- ½ of a 16-ounce package loose-pack frozen cut broccoli
- 1 stalk celery, sliced
- 2 green onions, sliced
- 2 tablespoons butter or margarine
- ½ teaspoon sugar
- ¼ teaspoon salt

In a large skillet, cook and stir broccoli, celery and green onion in hot butter over medium-high heat about 8 minutes or until tender-crisp. Stir in sugar and salt.

MIXED VEGETABLE-CHEESE PIE

Makes 6 servings

- 1 package (16 ounces) loose-pack frozen mixed broccoli, carrots and cauliflower
- 2 tablespoons butter or margarine
- ¼ teaspoon salt
- ¼ to ½ teaspoon dried dillweed
- 1 package refrigerated crescent rolls
- 2 beaten eggs
- 2 cups shredded Swiss cheese

In a large skillet, cook and stir vegetables in hot butter over medium-high heat for 6 to 8 minutes or until tender-crisp. Remove from heat; cut up larger vegetable pieces. Stir in salt and dillweed. Separate crescent rolls into 8 triangles. Place in an ungreased 10-inch pie plate, pressing over bottom and up sides to form a crust; press edges together to seal. Spoon vegetable mixture into crust; pour eggs over all. Sprinkle with cheese. Bake in a 375° oven for 20 minutes.

Menus

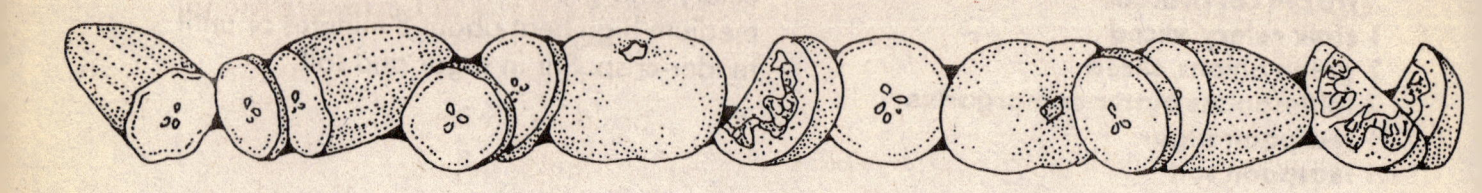

Beef Stroganoff*
Hot Cooked Noodles
Asparagus with Sesame Seed*
Tomato-Cucumber Salad*
Apple-Blueberry Crisp*

Shopping List:
- 1 pound beef tenderloin or sirloin steak
- 1½ pounds fresh asparagus
- 3 medium tomatoes
- 1 medium cucumber
- 2 cups sliced fresh mushrooms
- ½ cup chopped onion
- Lettuce leaves
- 1 cup fresh or frozen blueberries
- 1 tablespoon lemon juice
- 1 cup sour cream
- ½ cup butter or margarine
- Vanilla ice cream, optional
- ⅓ cup salad oil
- Noodles
- 1 can (21 ounces) apple pie filling
- ¼ cup quick-cooking rolled oats
- 6 tablespoons flour
- ¼ cup brown sugar
- 1 tablespoon granulated sugar
- 3 tablespoons white wine vinegar
- 2 teaspoons Worcestershire sauce
- 1 tablespoon sesame seed
- 1 teaspoon instant beef bouillon granules
- ½ teaspoon cinnamon
- ½ teaspoon dried basil
- ¼ teaspoon celery salt
- Paprika

Preparation Sequence:
1. Marinate tomatoes and cucumber in dressing mixture.
2. Prepare Apple-Blueberry Crisp.
3. Clean asparagus.
4. Brown meat in butter or margarine.
5. Cook asparagus.
6. Cook noodles according to package directions.
7. Complete preparation of Beef Stroganoff.
8. Arrange salads on salad plates.

Menus with Beef

*Steak and Onions**
*Hash Browns with Cheese**
Fresh Green Salad
Cantaloupe A La Mode

Shopping List:
- 4 beef cube steaks, about 1 pound each
- 1 large onion
- 1 package (12 ounces) frozen loose-pack hash brown potatoes
- 1 cup shredded Swiss or Cheddar cheese
- 2 tablespoons butter or margarine
- 5 tablespoons cooking oil
- ½ cup dry red or white wine
- ¼ cup soy sauce
- Garlic powder

Suggested Foods to Complete Menu:
- Green salad
- Cantaloupe
- Vanilla ice cream

Preparation Sequence:
1. Marinate cube steaks for Steak and Onions.
2. Prepare a green salad.
3. Cut cantaloupe.
4. Cook onion in butter.
5. Start cooking Hash Browns with Cheese.
6. Cook marinated steaks.

*Taco Salad**
Tortilla Chips
Banana Peppers
Vanilla Ice Cream
*Hot Butter-Pecan Sauce**

Shopping List:
- 1 pound ground beef
- 1 small onion
- 4 cups shredded lettuce
- 2 medium tomatoes
- ½ cup sour cream
- ¾ cup shredded Cheddar cheese
- ¼ cup butter or margarine
- Vanilla ice cream
- Tortilla chips
- ½ cup taco sauce
- Pitted ripe olives
- ¼ cup finely chopped pecans
- ½ cup sugar
- ½ teaspoon vanilla

Suggested Foods to Complete Menu:
- Banana peppers

Preparation Sequence:
1. Prepare ground beef for Taco Salad and chill.
2. Prepare Hot Butter-Pecan Sauce.
3. Assemble salads on individual salad plates.

Menus with Beef

Skillet Barbecues*
Potato Chips
Crisp Relishes   Dill Dip*
Fresh Sliced Peaches

Shopping List:
- 1 pound ground beef
- 1 medium onion
- ¾ cup sour cream
- ¼ cup mayonnaise or salad dressing
- 8 hamburger buns
- ½ cup catsup
- 1 teaspoon prepared mustard
- 1 teaspoon Worcestershire sauce
- ½ cup chili sauce
- 1 tablespoon vinegar
- 1 tablespoon instant minced onion
- 1 teaspoon dried dillweed
- 1 teaspoon dried parsley flakes
- ½ teaspoon sugar
- ¼ teaspoon celery salt
- ¼ teaspoon seasoning salt

Suggested Foods to Complete Menu:
- Potato chips
- Crisp relishes
- Fresh sliced peaches

Preparation Sequence:
1. Prepare Dill Dip and chill.
2. Combine ingredients for Skillet Barbecues and simmer.
3. Prepare relishes and sliced peaches.

Beef with Peppers and Tomatoes*
Hot Cooked Rice
Boston Lettuce Salad*
Fresh Pineapple

Shopping List:
- 1 pound beef tenderloin or sirloin steak
- 1 large green pepper
- 1 cup halved cherry tomatoes
- 2 small heads Boston lettuce
- 1 teaspoon snipped parsley
- 1 ounce shredded Cheddar cheese
- ½ cup sour cream
- 2 tablespoons cooking oil
- Rice
- ¼ cup Italian salad dressing
- 2 tablespoons mayonnaise or salad dressing
- 2 tablespoons soy sauce
- 2 tablespoons dry sherry
- 1 teaspoon cornstarch
- ½ teaspoon sugar

Suggested Foods to Complete Menu:
- Fresh pineapple

Preparation Sequence:
1. Cook rice according to package directions.
2. Combine dressing ingredients for Boston Lettuce Salad.
3. Prepare pineapple.
4. Prepare Beef with Peppers and Tomatoes.
5. Arrange salads on salad plates.

Menus with Chicken

Chicken Stir-Fry*
Hot Cooked Rice
Mixed Fruit with Sherbet*

Shopping List:
- 2 whole chicken breasts, skinned and boned
- 1½ cups sliced fresh mushrooms
- 2 stalks celery
- 6 green onions
- 1½ cups bean sprouts
- 2 slices gingerroot
- 1 package (10 ounces) frozen mixed fruit (in quick-thaw pouch)
- Orange sherbet
- 3 tablespoons cooking oil
- Rice
- ½ cup chicken broth
- 3 tablespoons cornstarch
- 1 teaspoon sugar
- 2 tablespoons creme de banana or orange liqueur
- 1 tablespoon dry white wine

Preparation Sequence:
1. Cut chicken and marinate in cornstarch-wine mixture.
2. Thaw fruit.
3. Cook rice according to package directions.
4. Combine fruit and liqueur, then chill until serving time.
5. Complete preparation of Chicken Stir-Fry.

Menus with Chicken

Chicken Salad in Croissants*
Swiss Cheese Soup*
Carrot Sticks
Apple Wedges

Shopping List:
- 2 cups diced cooked chicken
- 1 stalk celery
- Leaf lettuce
- 1 teaspoon snipped chives
- 3½ cups milk
- 6 slices processed Swiss cheese
- 3 tablespoons butter or margarine
- ½ cup mayonnaise or salad dressing
- 4 croissants
- 1 can (8¼ ounces) crushed pineapple
- 2 tablespoons sliced pimiento-stuffed olives
- ¼ cup chopped cashews
- ¼ cup flour
- 1 teaspoon instant chicken bouillon granules
- ¼ teaspoon paprika

Suggested Foods to Complete Menu:
- Carrot sticks
- Apple wedges

Preparation Sequence:
1. Combine ingredients for chicken salad and chill.
2. Prepare Swiss Cheese Soup.
3. Cut carrot sticks and apple wedges.
4. Assemble Chicken Salad in Croissants.

Menus with Chicken

*Cheesy Chicken and Noodles**
*Broccoli Sauté**
*Fruit and Yogurt Salad**
*Melon Melba**

Shopping List:
- 2 cups diced cooked chicken
- ½ of a 16-ounce package loose-pack frozen cut broccoli
- 1 stalk celery
- 2 green onions
- Leaf lettuce
- 1 teaspoon snipped parsley
- 2 medium apples
- 1 cup seedless green grapes
- 3 cups cubed honeydew melon
- 1 package (10 ounces) frozen raspberries (in quick-thaw pouch)
- ½ cup sour cream
- ½ cup strawberry yogurt
- ½ of an 8-ounce jar cheese spread
- 2 tablespoons butter or margarine
- 6 ounces medium noodles
- ½ cup mandarin orange sections
- ¼ cup flaked coconut
- 1 tablespoon flour
- 2 tablespoons plus ½ teaspoon sugar
- 1 teaspoon cornstarch
- 2 teaspoons instant chicken bouillon granules

Preparation Sequence:
1. Thaw fruit.
2. Cook noodles.
3. Prepare Fruit and Yogurt Salad.
4. Prepare sauce for Melon Melba.
5. Start Broccoli Sauté.
6. Complete preparation of Cheesy Chicken and Noodles.

Menus with Chicken

Butter-Broiled Chicken*
Corn with Mushrooms*
Romaine and Artichoke Toss*
Raspberry or Lemon Sherbet   Blueberry Sauce*

Shopping List:
- 8 to 10 chicken legs or thighs
- 1 package (10 ounces) frozen whole kernel corn
- 3 cups torn romaine
- 1 cup sliced fresh mushrooms
- 1 tablespoon snipped parsley
- 1 cup fresh or frozen blueberries
- 1 teaspoon lemon juice
- ½ cup butter or margarine
- ¼ cup mayonnaise or salad dressing
- 1 jar (6 ounces) marinated artichoke hearts
- 3 tablespoons sugar
- 2 teaspoons cornstarch
- 2 tablespoons tarragon vinegar
- 1 tablespoon anchovy paste
- 1 teaspoon Dijon-style mustard
- ¼ teaspoon seasoning salt
- ¼ teaspoon dried oregano
- Garlic powder
- Paprika

Suggested Foods to Complete Menu:
Raspberry or lemon sherbet

Preparation Sequence:
1. Prepare Blueberry Sauce and cool.
2. Preheat broiler and combine butter sauce for chicken.
3. Begin broiling chicken.
4. Prepare dressing for salad.
5. Combine salad ingredients.
6. Turn chicken.
7. Prepare Corn with Mushrooms.
8. Toss salad with dressing.

Menus with Chicken

Chicken Livers in Patty Shells*
Sautéed Carrots and Onions*
Fresh Greens   Tarragon-Oil Dressing*
Fresh Peach Compote*

Shopping List:
12 ounces chicken livers
2 slices bacon
1 pound carrots
1 medium onion
1½ cups sliced fresh mushrooms
3 medium peaches
2 tablespoons lemon juice
2 tablespoons frozen lemonade concentrate
4 frozen patty shells
⅓ cup milk
1 package (3 ounces) cream cheese
2 tablespoons butter or margarine
½ cup olive or salad oil
3 tablespoons tarragon vinegar
2 tablespoons light corn syrup
2 tablespoons orange liqueur
1 teaspoon flour
½ teaspoon sugar
1 teaspoon Dijon-style mustard
1 teaspoon Worcestershire sauce
1 clove garlic
1 teaspoon snipped chives

Suggested Foods to Complete Menu:
Fresh greens

Preparation Sequence:
1. Bake frozen patty shells.
2. Prepare Tarragon-Oil Dressing and chill.
3. Prepare Fresh Peach Compote and chill.
4. Fry bacon.
5. Start cooking Sautéed Carrots and Onions.
6. Prepare Chicken Livers in Patty Shells.
7. Toss fresh greens with dressing.

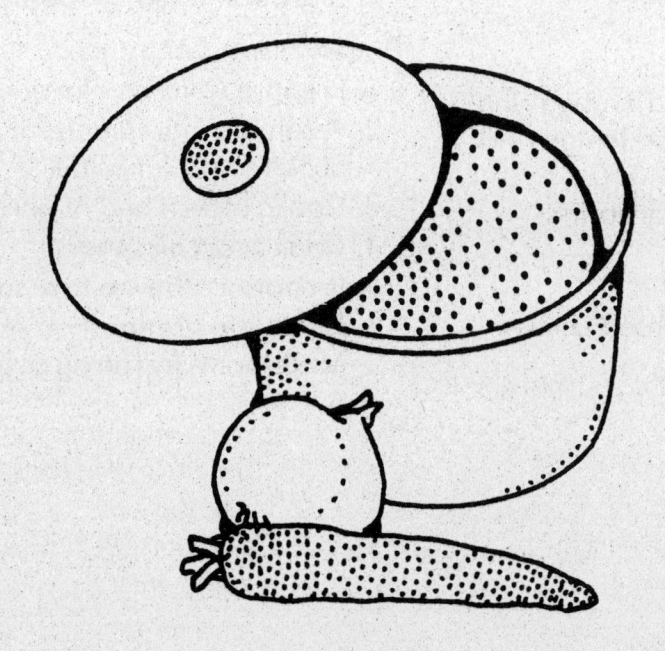

Menus with Chicken

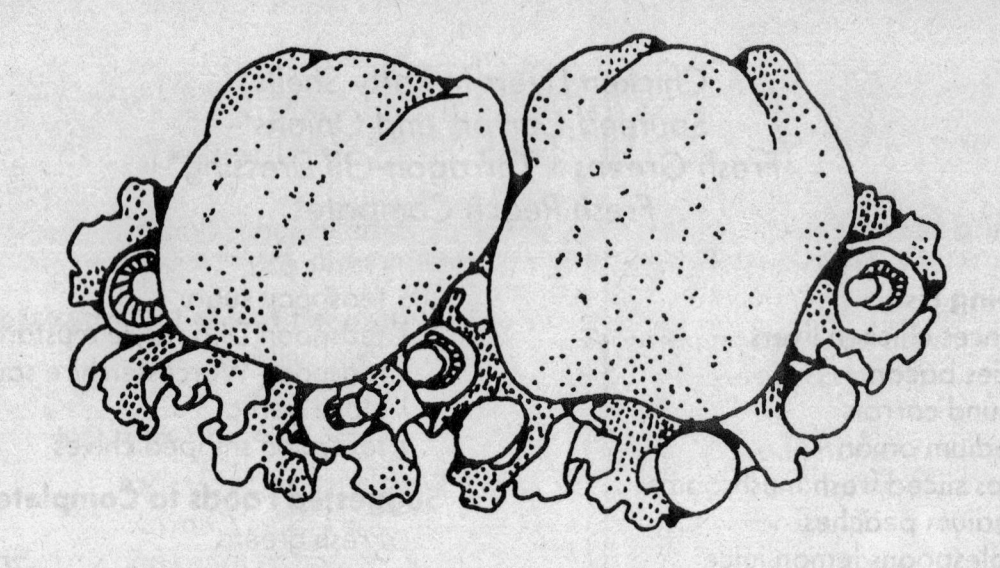

Chicken and Mushrooms in Tarragon Sauce*
Chicken-Flavored Rice*
Broccoli with Cashews*
Bananas Suzette*

Shopping List:
- 2 whole chicken breasts, skinned and boned
- 1 package (10 ounces) frozen broccoli spears
- 1½ cups sliced fresh mushrooms
- 4 firm ripe bananas
- ½ cup orange juice
- 1 teaspoon finely shredded orange rind
- 2 teaspoons finely shredded lemon rind
- 1 cup whipping cream
- 5 tablespoons butter or margarine
- 2 tablespoons cooking oil
- ⅔ cup long-grain rice
- 1 can (10¾ ounces) condensed chicken broth
- ¼ cup coarsely chopped cashews
- 2 teaspoons flour
- 6 tablespoons sugar
- 2 tablespoons orange liqueur
- 1 tablespoon instant chopped onion
- ¼ teaspoon dried tarragon

Preparation Sequence:
1. Prepare Chicken-Flavored Rice.
2. Assemble ingredients for Bananas Suzette and set aside.
3. Cook chicken and mushrooms in oil.
4. Cook broccoli spears.
5. Prepare cashew-butter sauce.
6. Complete preparation of Chicken and Mushrooms in Tarragon Sauce.

Menus with Fish

Clam Chowder*
Crisp Relishes   Avocado Dip*
Pound Cake   Fresh Sliced Strawberries

Shopping List:
- 1 can (6½ ounces) minced clams
- 2 slices bacon
- 3 cups frozen hash brown potatoes with onion and peppers
- 1 avocado
- 1 teaspoon lemon juice
- 2 cups light cream
- 1 cup plus 2 tablespoons milk
- ⅓ cup sour cream
- 2 tablespoons Italian salad dressing
- 2 tablespoons flour
- Garlic salt

Suggested Foods to Complete Menu:
- Crisp relishes
- Pound cake
- Fresh sliced strawberries

Preparation Sequence:
1. Start Clam Chowder.
2. Prepare relishes and strawberries.
3. Prepare Avocado Dip.
4. Complete preparation of chowder.

Oven-Fried Fish*   Tartar Sauce*
Corn on the Cob
Peas with Celery*
Coleslaw*
Watermelon

Shopping List:
- 1 pound fresh or frozen perch or other fish fillets
- 1 package (10 ounces) frozen peas
- 2 cups shredded cabbage
- ½ cup sliced celery
- ¼ cup shredded carrot
- ¼ cup finely chopped onion
- 1 lemon
- 1 egg
- ⅓ cup sour cream
- 2 tablespoons milk
- ½ cup butter or margarine
- ¾ cup mayonnaise or salad dressing
- 3 tablespoons pickle relish
- ¼ cup fine dry seasoned bread crumbs
- 2 tablespoons flour
- 2 tablespoons sugar
- 2 tablespoons vinegar
- ¼ teaspoon seasoned salt
- ¼ teaspoon dried thyme
- Garlic powder

Suggested Foods to Complete Menu:
- Corn on the cob
- Watermelon

Preparation Sequence:
1. Prepare Coleslaw and chill.
2. Prepare Tartar Sauce and chill.
3. Coat fish with egg and crumb mixture.
4. Cook corn.
5. Prepare Peas with Celery.
6. Bake fish.

Menus with Fish

Broiled Shrimp Kebabs*
Pasta and Pea Pods*
Bananas with Rum Cream*

Shopping List:
- 1 pound fresh or frozen large shrimp in shells
- 1 package (6 ounces) frozen pea pods
- 1 carrot, optional
- 4 small bananas
- 4 lemon slices
- 1 egg
- ¼ cup grated Romano cheese
- ½ cup butter or margarine
- ¼ cup cooking oil
- ½ of a 4-ounce container frozen whipped dessert topping
- 8 ounces mostaccioli
- ¼ cup brown sugar
- 1 tablespoon dark rum
- Chocolate curls, optional
- 4 whole allspice
- 3 garlic cloves
- 1 teaspoon dried tarragon
- 1 teaspoon dried oregano
- Bay leaves, optional

Preparation Sequence:
1. Peel and devein shrimp.
2. Combine ingredients for marinade; add shrimp.
3. Prepare Rum Cream.
4. Cook mostaccioli and pea pods.
5. Thread shrimp on skewers and broil.
6. Complete preparation of Pasta and Pea Pods.

Broiled Salmon Steaks*
Oven Potatoes with Dill*
Green Beans Amandine*
Peach Cobbler*

Shopping List:
- 1 pound fresh or frozen salmon steaks, cut 1 inch thick
- 1 pound new potatoes
- 1 package (9 ounces) frozen whole green beans
- 1 tablespoon plus 2 teaspoons lemon juice
- 1 tablespoon milk
- 6 tablespoons plus 1 teaspoon butter or margarine
- 1 teaspoon cooking oil
- 1 can (16 ounces) sliced peaches
- ½ cup biscuit mix
- 5 tablespoons sugar
- 2 teaspoons cornstarch
- ¼ cup slivered almonds
- 1 teaspoon Worcestershire sauce
- ½ teaspoon dried dillweed
- ½ teaspoon cinnamon

Preparation Sequence:
1. Prepare Oven Potatoes with Dill.
2. Prepare Peach Cobbler.
3. Start preparation of Green Beans Amandine.
4. Prepare broiled Salmon Steaks.
5. Combine green beans and almond-butter.

Menus with Fish

Halibut with Mushrooms*
Saffron Rice*
Cucumber-Pea Salad*
Strawberries with Cream*

Shopping List:
- 1 pound fresh or frozen halibut or other fish steaks, cut 1 inch thick
- 1½ cups sliced fresh mushrooms
- 3 cups torn lettuce
- 1 small cucumber
- 1 cup frozen peas
- 2 tablespoons snipped parsley
- 2 cups fresh strawberries
- 1 lemon
- ¼ cup sour cream
- ¼ cup whipping cream
- ¼ cup butter or margarine
- ⅓ cup salad oil
- ½ of a 4-ounce container frozen whipped dessert topping
- ⅔ cup long-grain rice
- ½ of a 3-ounce can French-fried onions
- 2 tablespoons plus 1 teaspoon sugar
- 2 tablespoons vinegar
- ¼ teaspoon dry mustard
- ¼ teaspoon paprika
- ¼ teaspoon dried dillweed
- ¼ teaspoon dried tarragon
- ⅛ teaspoon saffron
- ⅛ teaspoon cinnamon
- Seasoning salt

Preparation Sequence:
1. Prepare Saffron Rice.
2. Combine strawberries and sugar, then chill.
3. Prepare topping mixture for Strawberries with Cream.
4. Start preparation of Cucumber-Pea Salad.
5. Prepare Halibut with Mushrooms.
6. Toss salad with dressing.

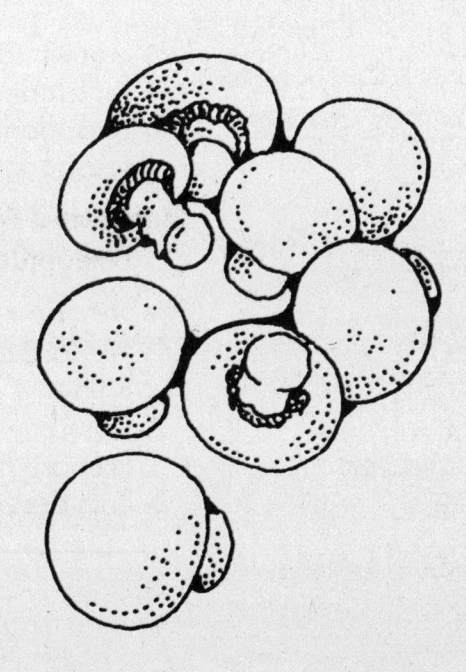

Menus with Fish

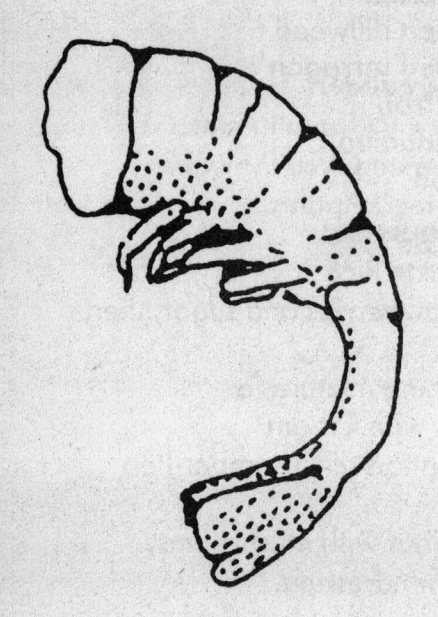

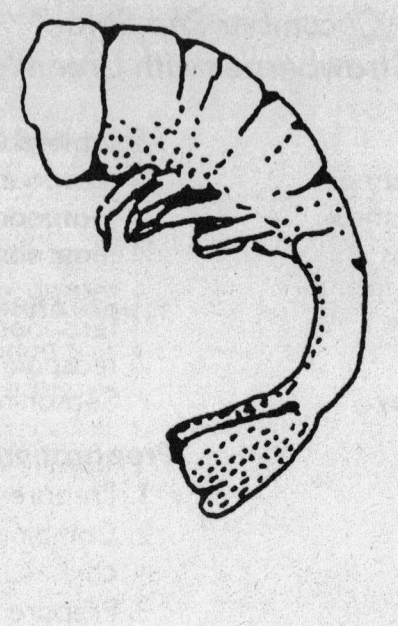

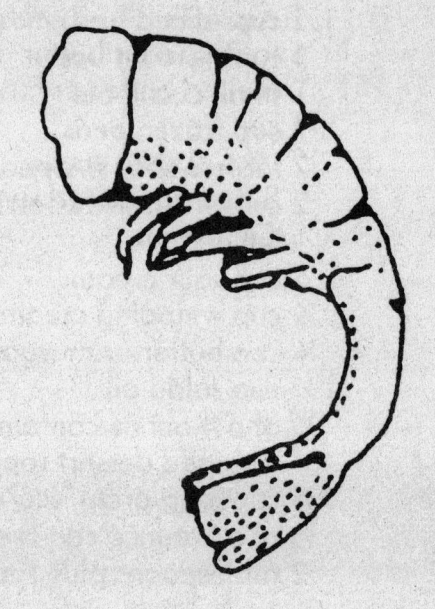

Fried Rice with Shrimp*
Vinaigrette Salad*
Pineapple Sherbet

Shopping List:
- 1 cup cooked shrimp
- 1 cup frozen peas
- 1 cup sliced green onion
- 1 medium green pepper
- 1 small green pepper
- 3 cups torn romaine
- 8 cherry tomatoes
- 1 teaspoon snipped chives
- 4 eggs
- 3 cups cooked rice
- ⅓ cup plus 3 tablespoons salad or cooking oil
- ¼ cup white wine vinegar
- 4 teaspoons sugar
- ½ teaspoon dry mustard
- ½ teaspoon dried basil

Suggested Foods to Complete Menu:
Pineapple sherbet

Preparation Sequence:
1. Prepare dressing for Vinaigrette Salad.
2. Combine salad ingredients.
3. Prepare Fried Rice with Shrimp.
4. Toss dressing with salad.

Menus with Pork

*German Oven Pancake**
Brown-and-Serve Sausage Links
*Sautéed Apples**
Honeydew Melon with Lime Wedges

Shopping List:
- 4 medium apples
- 6 eggs
- 1 cup milk
- 6 tablespoons butter or margarine
- Melted butter or margarine
- 1 cup flour
- 2 tablespoons sugar
- Sifted powdered sugar
- Cinnamon

Suggested Foods to Complete Menu:
- Brown-and-Serve sausage links
- Honeydew melon
- Lime wedges

Preparation Sequence:
1. Cut honeydew melon and lime.
2. Prepare German Oven Pancake.
3. Prepare Sautéed Apples.
4. Brown sausage links.

*Tuna-Shoestring Salad**
Cherry Tomatoes
Sweet Pickles
*Peach Sundae Crunch**

Shopping List:
- 1 can (9¼ ounces) tuna
- 2 stalks celery
- 2 carrots
- ½ small onion
- Lettuce leaves
- 1 teaspoon lemon juice
- Vanilla ice cream
- 2 tablespoons butter or margarine
- ¾ cup mayonnaise or salad dressing
- 1 can (16 ounces) peach slices
- 1½ cups shoestring potatoes
- 8 pitted ripe olives
- ¼ cup quick-cooking rolled oats
- ¼ cup brown sugar
- 1 teaspoon prepared mustard
- ¼ teaspoon cinnamon

Suggested Foods to Complete Menu:
- Cherry tomatoes
- Sweet pickles

Preparation Sequence:
1. Combine ingredients for Tuna-Shoestring Salad and chill.
2. Prepare crunch mixture for Peach Sundae Crunch.
3. Just before serving, toss tuna salad with shoestring potatoes.

Menus with Pork

Canadian Bacon-Asparagus Stack-Ups*
Carrot Sticks
Ambrosia-Nut Dessert*

Shopping List:
- 8 slices Canadian-style bacon
- 1 package (10 ounces) frozen asparagus spears
- 1 cup fresh pineapple chunks
- 1 cup seedless green grapes
- ½ cup fresh blueberries
- 2 eggs
- 1⅔ cups milk
- ¼ cup butter or margarine
- 4 English muffins
- 2 tablespoons shredded coconut
- 1 tablespoon finely chopped pecans
- 2 tablespoons flour
- ¼ teaspoon curry powder
- Paprika

Suggested Foods to Complete Menu:
Carrot sticks

Preparation Sequence:
1. Toast coconut with pecans and butter.
2. Combine fruits for Ambrosia-Nut Dessert.
3. Prepare carrot sticks.
4. Prepare Canadian Bacon-Asparagus Stack-Ups.
5. Just before serving, toss fruit with toasted coconut mixture.

Cream of Tomato Soup
Mixed Vegetable-Cheese Pie*
Vanilla Ice Cream
Chocolate-Peanut Sauce*

Shopping List:
- 1 package (16 ounces) loose-pack frozen mixed broccoli, carrots and cauliflower
- 2 cups shredded Swiss Cheese
- 2 eggs
- ¾ cup milk
- 2 tablespoons butter or margarine
- Vanilla ice cream
- 1 package refrigerated crescent rolls
- ½ cup chunk-style peanut butter
- 2 squares semi-sweet chocolate
- ⅓ cup sugar
- ½ teaspoon dried dillweed

Suggested Foods to Complete Menu:
Cream of tomato soup

Preparation Sequence:
1. Prepare Mixed Vegetable-Cheese Pie.
2. Prepare Chocolate-Peanut Sauce.
3. Heat cream of tomato soup.

Menus with Pork

*Mostaccioli Bake**
*Seasoned Italian Green Beans**
*Garlic Bread**
*Fresh Fruit with Marmalade Cream**

Shopping List:
- 8 ounces bulk Italian sausage
- 1 package (9 ounces) frozen Italian green beans
- 1 tablespoon snipped parsley
- 3 cups mixed fresh fruit
- ½ cup cream-style cottage cheese
- ½ cup plus ⅓ cup sour cream
- 1 cup shredded Mozzarella cheese
- ¼ cup butter or margarine
- 6 ounces mostaccioli
- 8 slices Italian bread
- 1 cup meatless spaghetti sauce
- 2 tablespoons regular onion soup mix
- 1 tablespoon chopped pimiento
- 1 tablespoon orange marmalade
- ¼ teaspoon dried oregano
- ¼ teaspoon garlic powder
- Paprika
- Nutmeg

Preparation Sequence:
1. Prepare Mostaccioli Bake.
2. Spread bread with garlic butter and wrap in foil.
3. Combine ingredients for Marmalade Cream.
4. Prepare Seasoned Italian Green Beans.
5. Heat bread.
6. Prepare fresh fruit.

Menus with Pork

Spinach-Bacon Toss*
Cheese Plate
Assorted Crackers
Almond-Fudge Bars*

Shopping List:
- 6 slices bacon
- 6 cups torn spinach
- 1 cup sliced fresh mushrooms
- 1 small onion
- 4 eggs
- ½ cup butter or margarine
- ½ cup salad oil
- 1⅓ cups sugar
- ¾ cup flour
- 2 squares unsweetened chocolate
- ½ cup semi-sweet chocolate pieces
- ⅓ cup chopped almonds
- 3 tablespoons vinegar
- 2 teaspoons prepared mustard
- ½ teaspoon celery seed
- ½ teaspoon almond extract

Suggested Foods to Complete Menu:
- Assorted cheeses
- Assorted crackers

Preparation Sequence:
1. Prepare dressing for salad and chill.
2. Prepare Almond-Fudge Bars.
3. Fry bacon.
4. Arrange cheese plate and crackers.
5. Combine salad ingredients.
6. Toss salad with dressing.

Menus with Pork

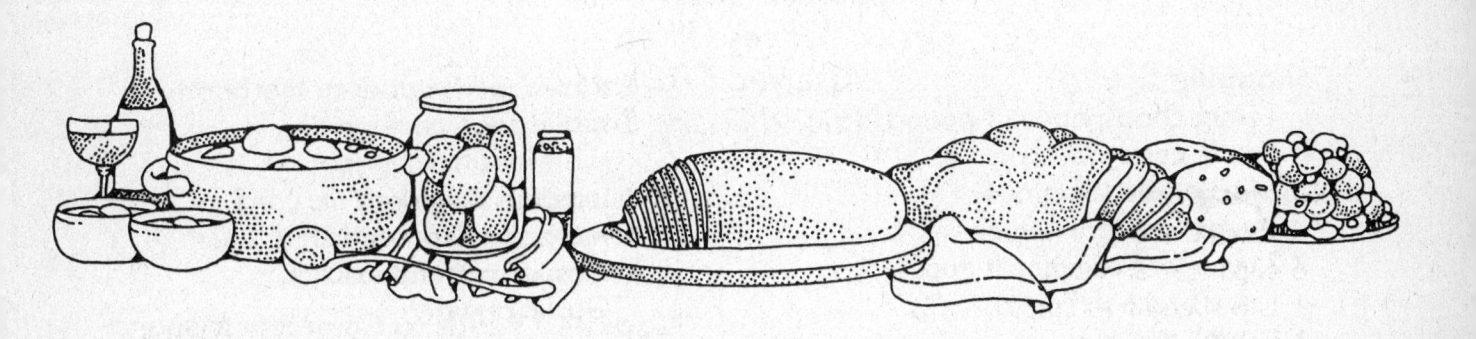

Broiled Ham with Apricot Glaze*
Cauliflower with Almond-Dill Butter*
Avocado-Orange Salad*
Stirred Rice Pudding*

Shopping List:
- 1 1-pound fully cooked center-cut ham slice
- 1 package (10 ounces) frozen cauliflower
- 1 avocado
- 1 small onion
- Bibb lettuce
- 2 oranges
- 1 tablespoon orange or pineapple juice
- 2 eggs
- 1 cup milk
- 2 tablespoons butter or margarine
- 1 cup cooked rice
- ½ cup clear French salad dressing
- ¼ cup raisins
- 2 tablespoons slivered almonds
- 2 tablespoons apricot preserves
- ¼ cup sugar
- 1 teaspoon vanilla
- ½ teaspoon Dijon-style mustard
- ¼ teaspoon dried dillweed
- Cinnamon

Preparation Sequence:
1. Prepare Stirred Rice Pudding and chill.
2. Arrange oranges, avocado and onion on salad plates, then chill.
3. Cook cauliflower and prepare Almond-Dill Butter.
4. Broil ham and prepare glaze.
5. Drizzle salad dressing over salads.

Menus with Pork

Pork Chops with Brown Rice*
Broiled Tomatoes*
Mixed Green Salad*   *Blue Cheese Dressing**
Apple Pie

Shopping List:
  4 pork chops, about 1 pound
  1 stalk celery
  2 large ripe tomatoes
  2 cups torn leaf lettuce
  2 cups torn romaine lettuce
  1 cup broccoli florets
  1 small zucchini
  4 radishes
  2 green onions
  1 package (4⅝ ounces) quick-cooking brown and wild rice mix with mushrooms
  ¾ cup soft bread crumbs
  1¼ cups sour cream
  ¼ cup buttermilk
  ¼ cup grated Parmesan cheese
  ¼ cup crumbled blue cheese
  2 tablespoons butter or margarin
  1 tablespoon cooking oil
  1 tablespoon vinegar
  1 teaspoon sugar
  ½ teaspoon Worcestershire sauce
  ¼ teaspoon dried basil
  Garlic powder

Suggested Foods to Complete Menu:
Apple pie

Preparation Sequence:
1. Start preparation of Pork Chops with Brown Rice.
2. Prepare Blue Cheese Dressing.
3. Combine ingredients for Mixed Green Salad.
4. Prepare Broiled Tomatoes.
5. Toss dressing with salad.

Menus with Pork

Jambalaya*
Fresh Greens   Honey-French Dressing*
Parmesan-Parsley Rolls*
Chocolate Cake with Broiled Icing*

Shopping List:
- 1 cup cubed fully cooked ham
- 1 cup cooked shrimp
- 1 medium green pepper
- 2 green onions
- 1 onion slice
- 1 tablespoon snipped parsley
- ½ cup butter or margarine
- 2 tablespoons whipping cream
- 2 tablespoons grated Parmesan cheese
- ⅓ cup salad oil
- ¾ cup long-grain rice
- 1 package refrigerated crescent rolls
- 1 frozen unfrosted chocolate cake (1 layer)
- 1 can (28 ounces) tomatoes
- ⅓ cup vinegar
- ⅓ cup catsup
- ⅓ cup honey
- ¼ cup brown sugar
- ½ teaspoon sugar
- ¼ cup chopped nuts
- 1 teaspoon instant beef bouillon granules
- 1 bay leaf
- ½ teaspoon celery seed
- ¼ teaspoon dry mustard
- Hot pepper sauce

Suggested Foods to Complete Menu:
Fresh greens

Preparation Sequence:
1. Prepare Honey-French Dressing and chill.
2. Combine icing ingredients and spread over frozen cake.
3. Start Jambalaya and let simmer until rice is tender.
4. Prepare Parmesan-Parsley Rolls and bake.
5. Stir shrimp and green pepper into Jambalaya.
6. Toss fresh greens with dressing.

Menus with Pork

Barbecue-Style Pork Chops*
Hash Browns Au Gratin*
Mixed Vegetable Salad*
Melon in Citrus Sauce*

Shopping List:
- 4 pork chops, about 1 pound
- 1 package (12 ounces) frozen loose-pack hash brown potatoes
- 1 box (10 ounces) frozen mixed vegetables
- 4 onion slices
- ½ cup halved cherry tomatoes
- Lettuce leaves
- 2 cups cubed honeydew melon
- 2 cups cubed cantaloupe
- 4 lemon slices
- ¼ cup orange juice
- 3 tablespoons lime juice
- 1 cup whipping cream
- ¼ cup shredded American cheese
- ½ cup tomato juice
- ¼ cup catsup
- ½ cup Green Goddess salad dressing
- 2 tablespoons sliced pitted ripe olives
- ¼ cup granulated sugar
- 1 tablespoon brown sugar
- 1 tablespoon vinegar
- 1 teaspoon Worcestershire sauce
- ¼ teaspoon chili powder

Preparation Sequence:
1. Cook frozen mixed vegetables.
2. Bake pork chops with lemon and onion slices.
3. Combine ingredients for Hash Browns Au Gratin.
4. Prepare barbecue sauce, then pour over chops.
5. Place chops and potatoes in the oven.
6. Combine mixed vegetables with salad dressing and chill.
7. Prepare Melon in Citrus Sauce.
8. Complete preparation of Mixed Vegetable Salad.

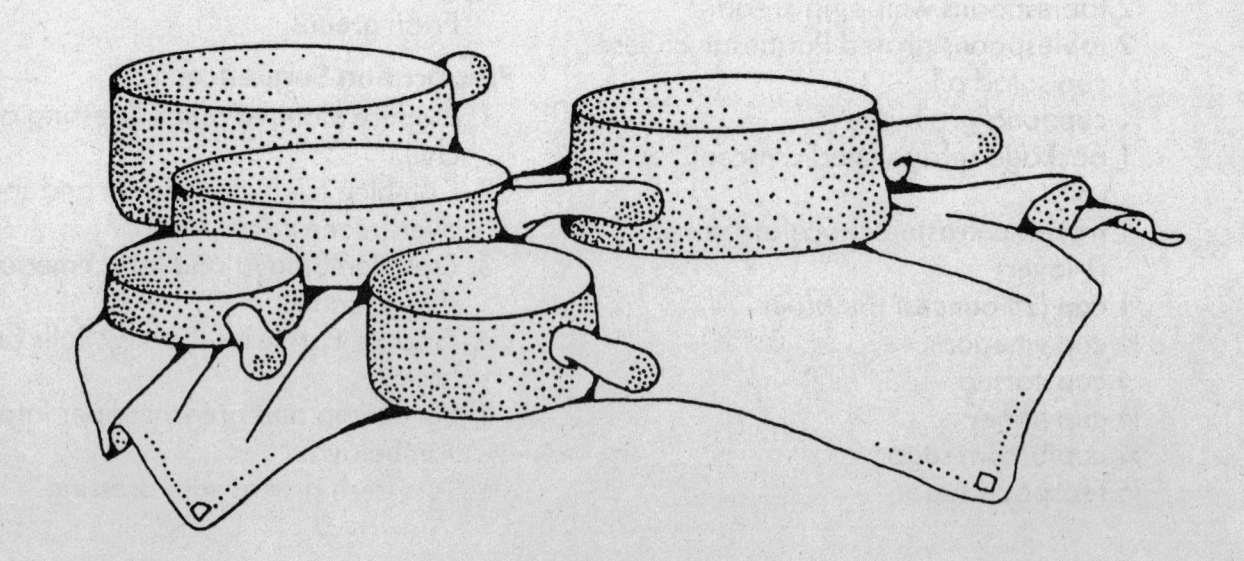

NOTES

NOTES